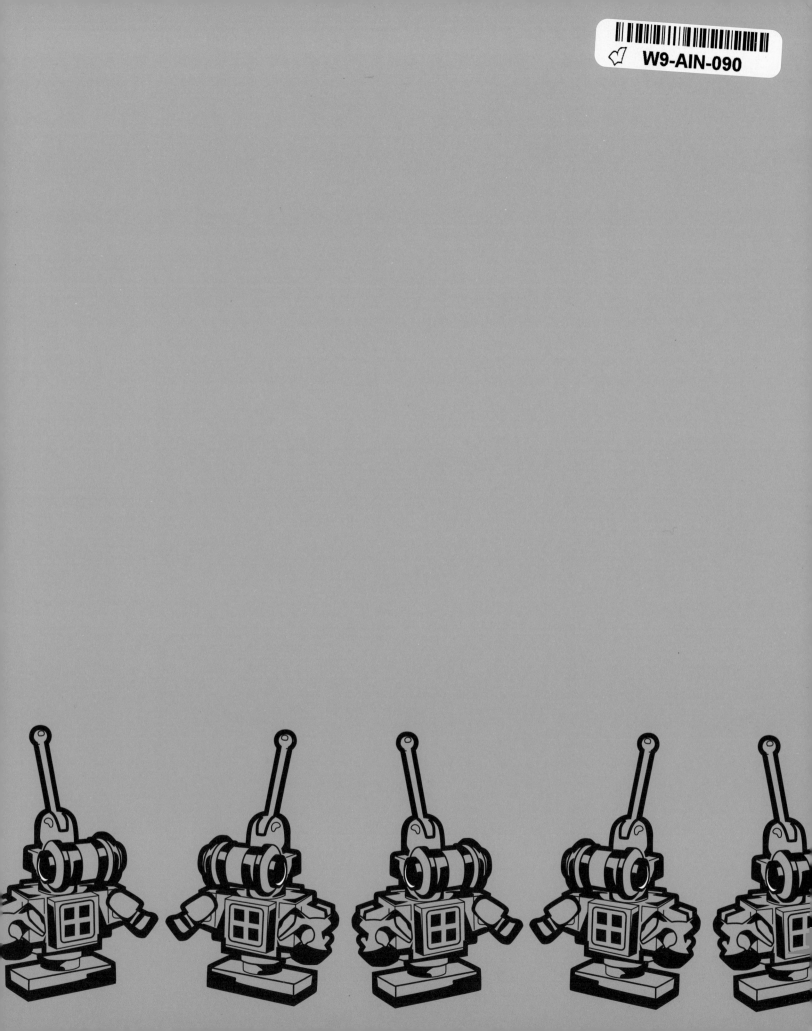

The LEGO® Adventure Book

Robots, Planes, Cities & More!

Megan H. Rothrock

no starch
press

San Francisco

The LEGO® Adventure Book, Volume 3: Robots, Planes, Cities & More!
Copyright © 2015 by Megan H. Rothrock.

First printing

Printed in China

19 18 17 16 15   1 2 3 4 5 6 7 8 9

ISBN-10: 1-59327-610-9
ISBN-13: 978-1-59327-610-2

Publisher: William Pollock
Production Editor: Serena Yang
Interior Design: Megan H. Rothrock
Featured Cover Model: Eco Villa by Birgitte Jonsgard
Title Page Illustration: Brian Ellis
Additional Photography: Chris Salt (Chapter 3) and Mark Stafford (Chapters 1 and 6)
LDD Models: Megan H. Rothrock (Chapters 3, 8, and 10) and James Shields (Chapter 3)
Proofreaders: Paula L. Fleming and Laurel Chun

For information on distribution, translations, or bulk sales,
please contact No Starch Press, Inc. directly:
No Starch Press, Inc.
245 8th Street, San Francisco, CA 94103
phone: 415.863.9900; info@nostarch.com; http://www.nostarch.com/

Library of Congress Cataloging-in-Publication Data
The Library of Congress Control Number for this volume is 2012033902.

Production Date: 6/8/2015
Plant & Location: Printed by Everbest Printing (Guangzhou, China), Co. Ltd
Job/Batch #: 54145-0 / EPC 707065

CONTENTS

Megs and the CCC

Giant LEGO Bricks

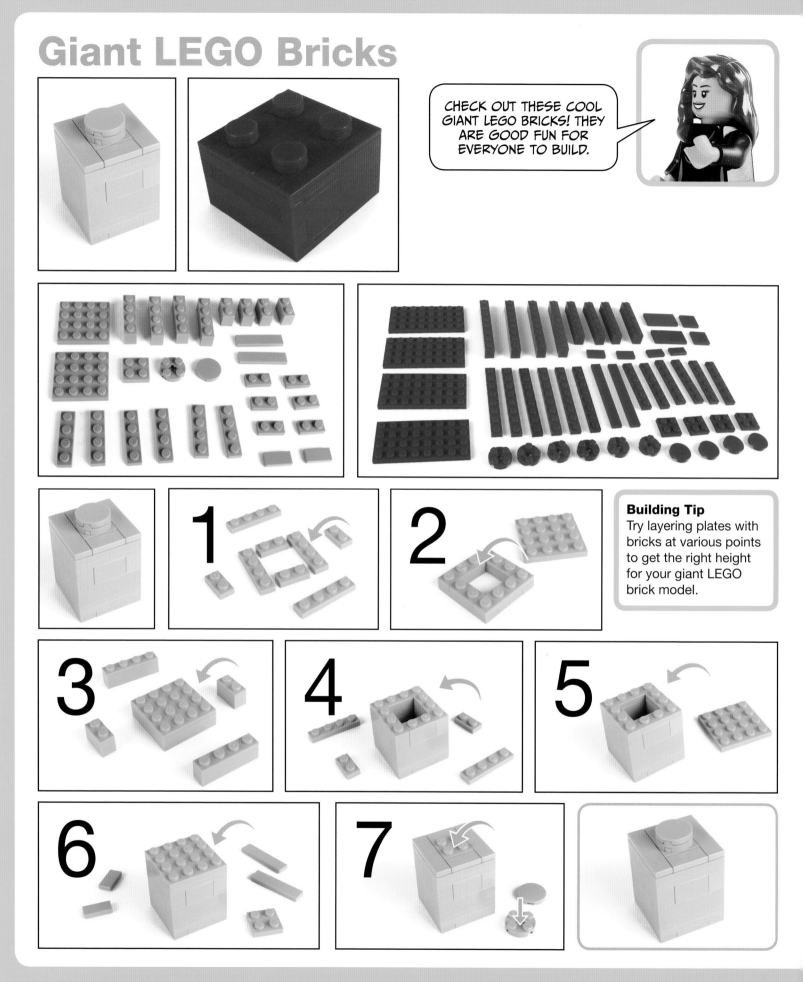

CHECK OUT THESE COOL GIANT LEGO BRICKS! THEY ARE GOOD FUN FOR EVERYONE TO BUILD.

1

2

Building Tip
Try layering plates with bricks at various points to get the right height for your giant LEGO brick model.

3

4

5

6

7

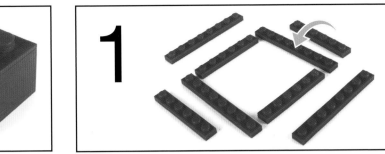

1

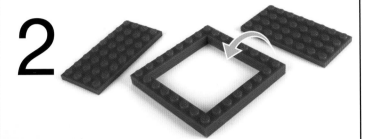

Building Tip
Using larger plates that span the width of your brick model will add strength to your build and reduce the complexity of your model.

2

3

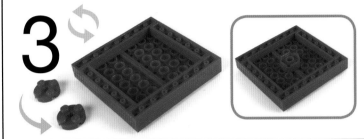

4

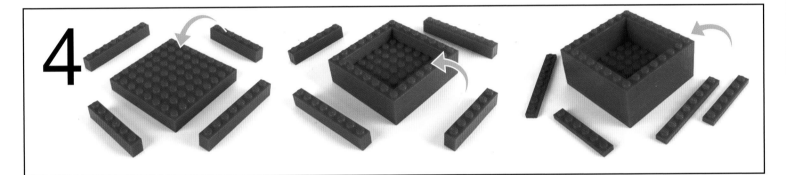

5

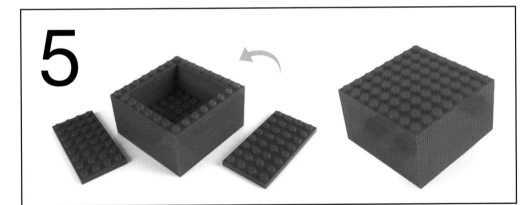

BUILDING JOURNAL

These large LEGO bricks are quite fun! But I can't help feeling that something is amiss in this amazing place. Only time will tell.

6

Other Destructörs

The Mummy D–Dögg KylliKyat Vakuum Big Other

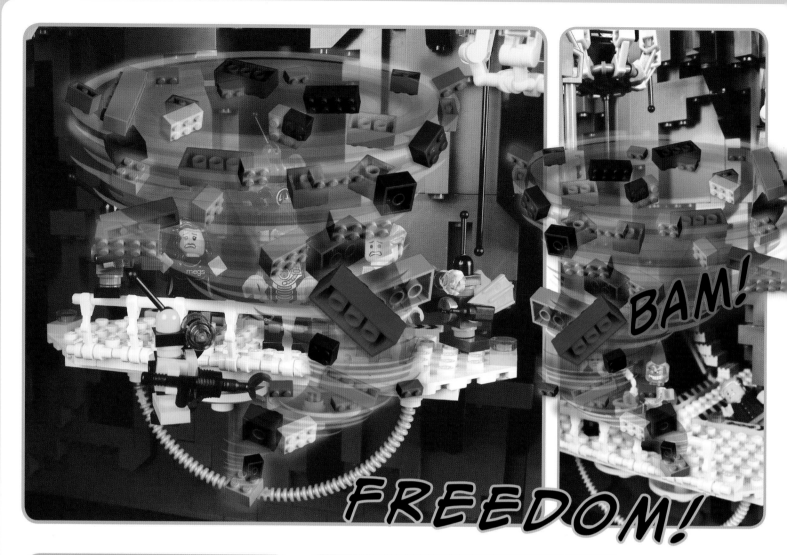

BAM!

FREEDOM!

WAKE UP, MEGS!

I THINK SHE'LL BE OKAY.

BUT THANKS TO HER, ALL THE LUNATICS ARE OUT OF ARKHAM.

I THOUGHT IT WAS AZKABAN?

MORDOR?

IT'S JUST A JAIL.

AYE, LIKE A DESERTED ISLAND. OR A CAVE. IN THE DARK. WITH NO OCEAN. *YARHH.*

HE ESCAPED? HE'S OUT THERE AGAIN?

AND HE FREED THE OTHER DESTRUCTORS, TOO. THAT MUST HAVE BEEN HIS PLAN ALL ALONG. I THOUGHT WE CAUGHT HIM TOO EASILY. WE SHOULD HAVE BEEN MORE SUSPICIOUS.

IT WILL TAKE HARD WORK, BUT IF WE WORK TOGETHER, WE CAN TURN THIS AROUND. WE CAN SAVE THE LEGO WORLD FROM THE DESTRUCTORS.

RIGHT, WE HAVE THE GREATEST TEAM OF CONSTRUCTIVE HEROES EVER ASSEMBLED HERE. AND I'M A HANDSOME GENIUS. THAT COULD HELP.

I'LL BUILD A CONTAINMENT SYSTEM.

I'LL BUILD A SPACESHIP!

BRILLIANT. I'LL HELP!

Great Times in Dordrecht

Patrick Bosman

Profession: Historic Preservation Advisor

Nationality: Dutch

Website: *www.flickr.com/photos/patrick-bosman/*

17th-Century Dutch House

MY HOUSE IS A RATHER COMPLEX BUILDING, SO PAY CLOSE ATTENTION TO THE STEPS AND DON'T WORK TOO FAST. KEEP AN EYE OUT FOR DETAILS AND HIDDEN FEATURES AS WELL. ONLY ADVANCED LEGO BUILDERS SHOULD TRY TO TACKLE THIS BUILD!

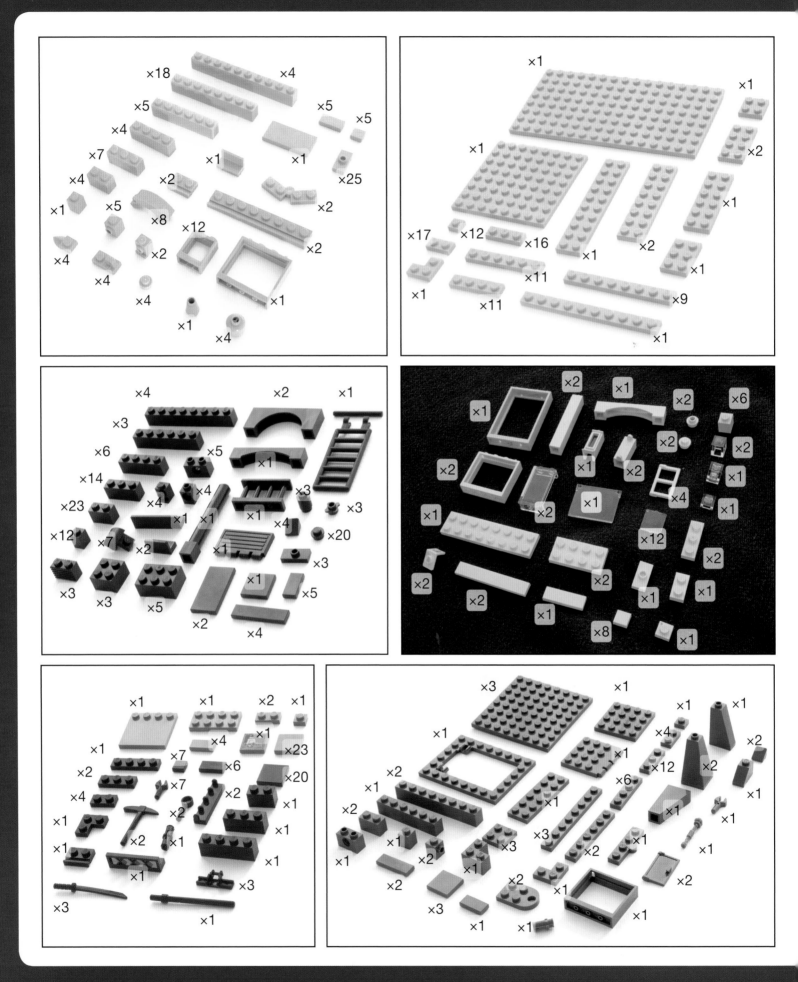

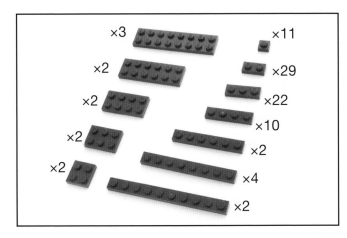

×3   ×11
×2   ×29
×2   ×22
×2   ×10
×2   ×2
×2   ×4
×2

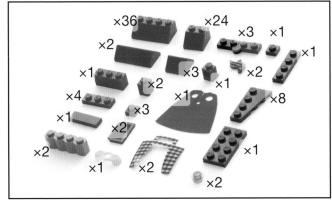

×36   ×24   ×3   ×1
×2   ×1
×1   ×3   ×1
×4   ×2   ×1   ×8
×1   ×3
×2   ×2   ×1
×1   ×2   ×2

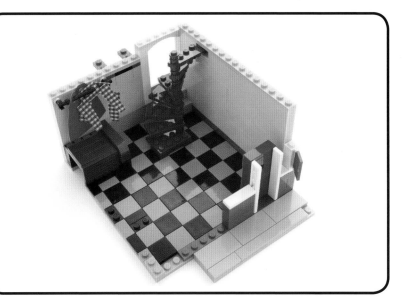

×3   ×3   ×1   ×1
×2
×1   ×1   ×7
×1   ×1
×1   ×3   ×1   ×1
×3   ×3   ×1   ×1   ×2
×1   ×2   ×4
×2   ×1   ×1   ×2
×2   ×2   ×7   ×1   ×1   ×3

Building Tip

It's a good idea to work out the footprint of your structure before you start building. Planning ahead will help building go more smoothly once you start adding stories. Also, incorporating a free-swing hinge, as shown in step 2, let you open your building with ease.

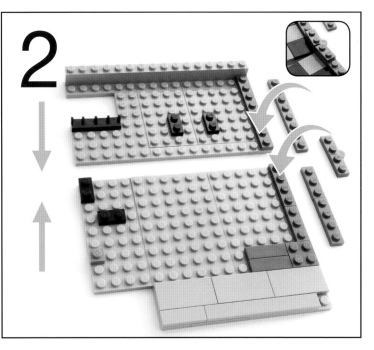

1

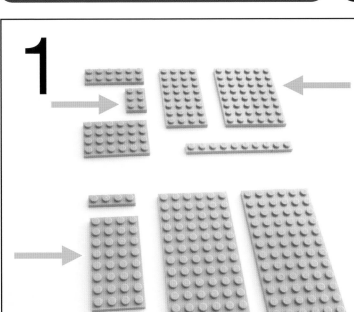

2

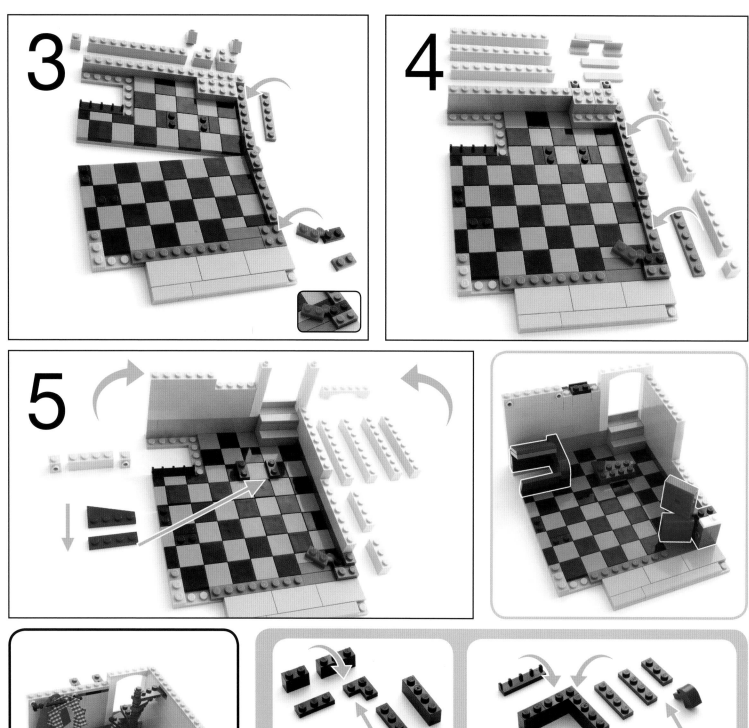

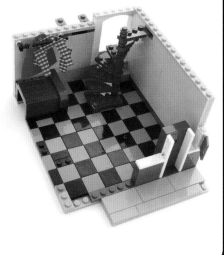

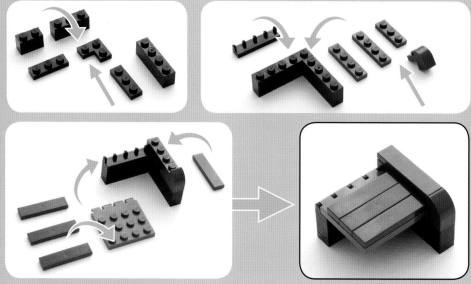

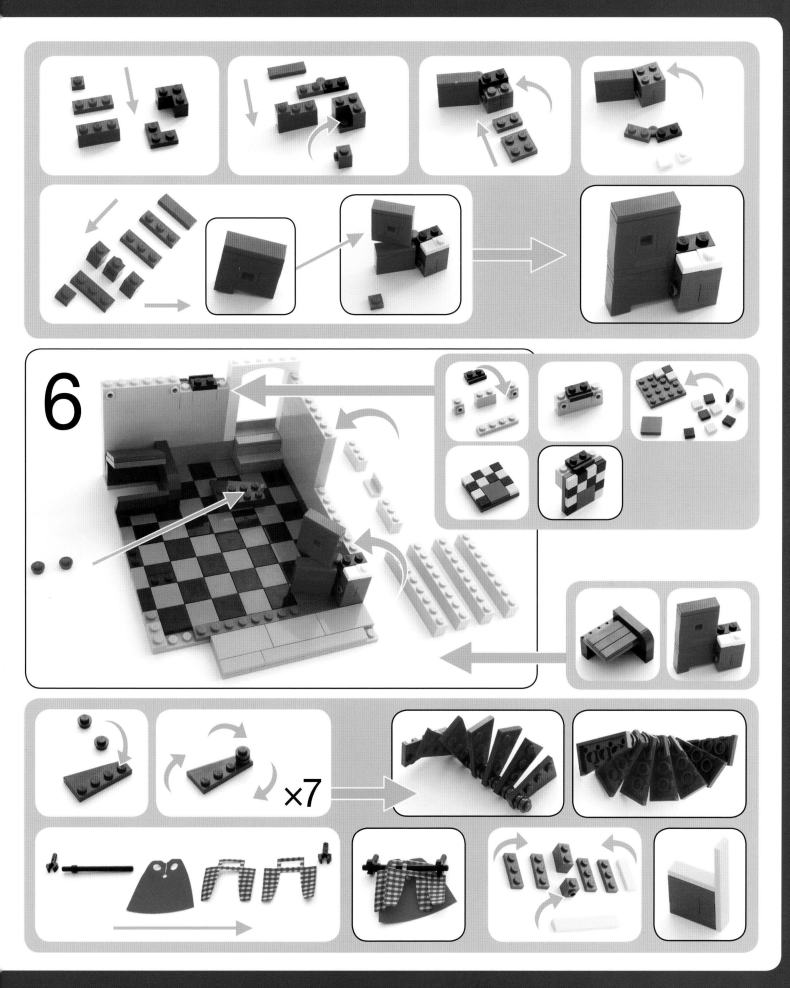

7

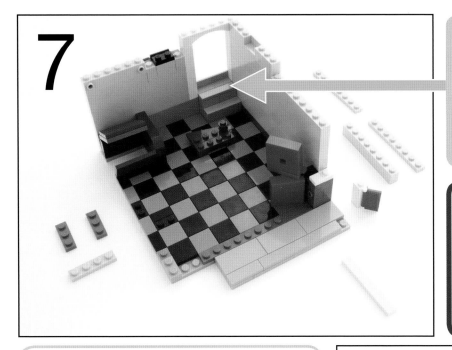

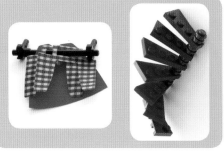

Building Tip
When building a staircase, think about how it will attach to the rest of your building. Here, Patrick built negative space into the side wall to provide enough space for the top step.

8

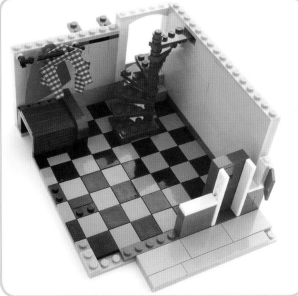

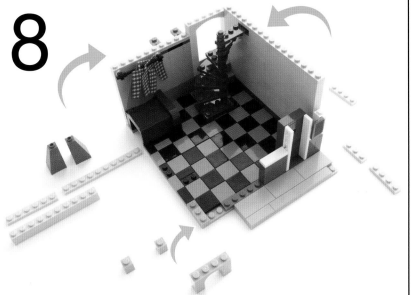

9

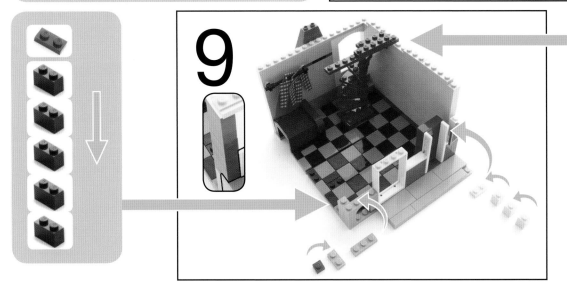

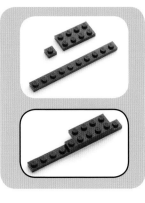

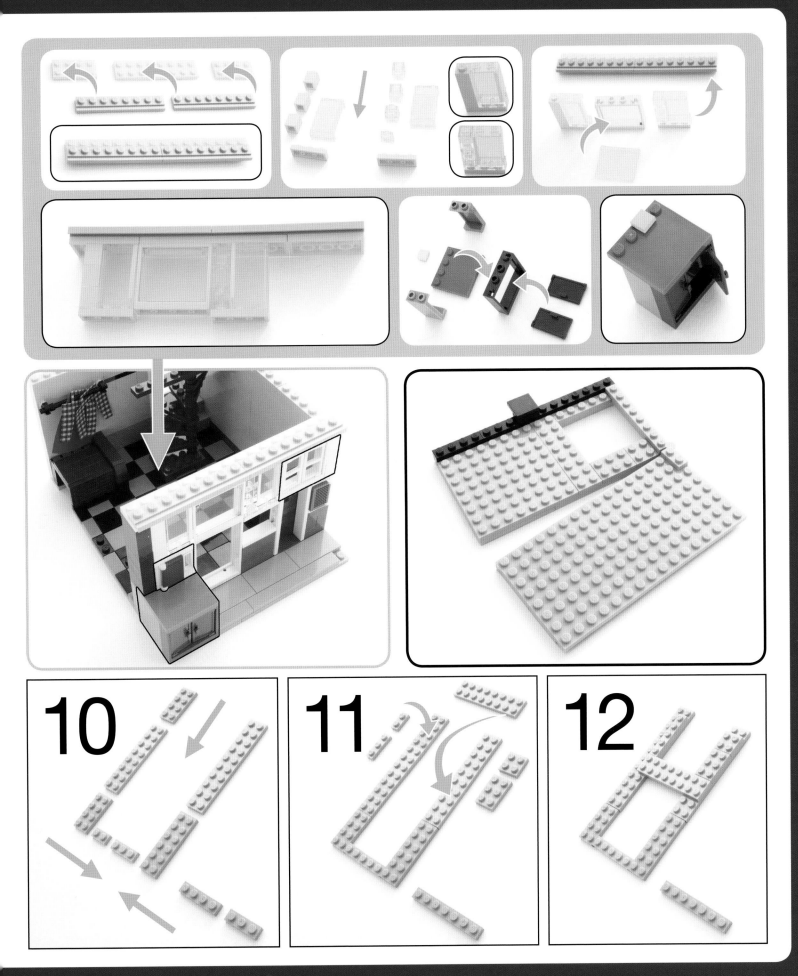

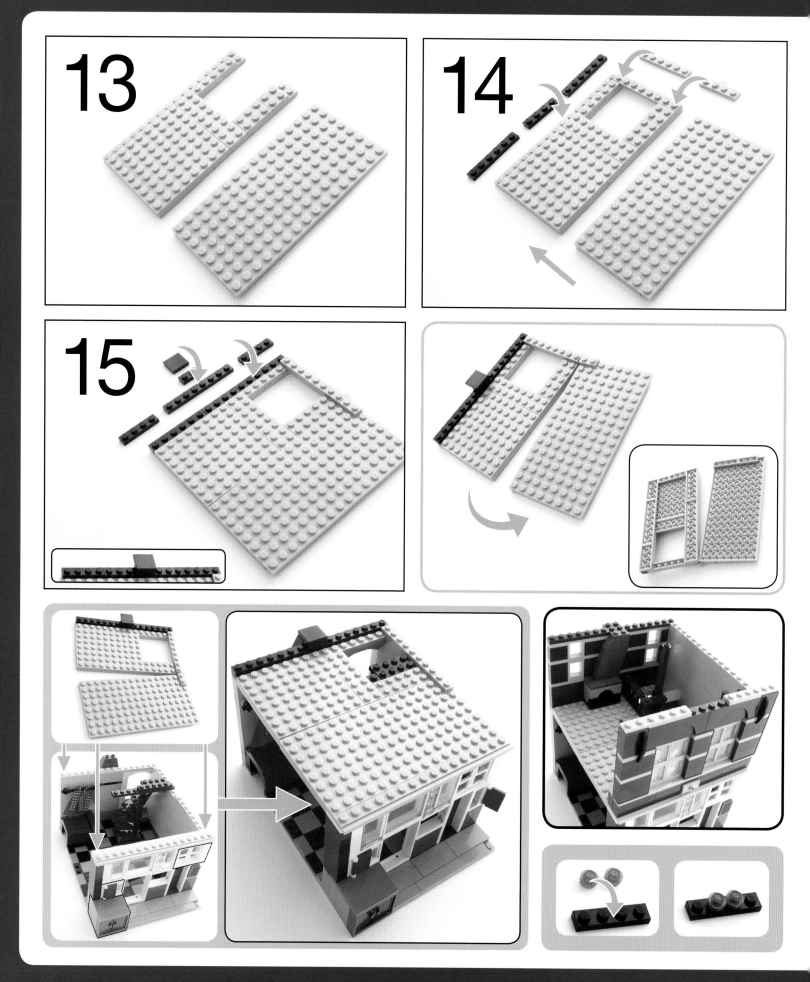

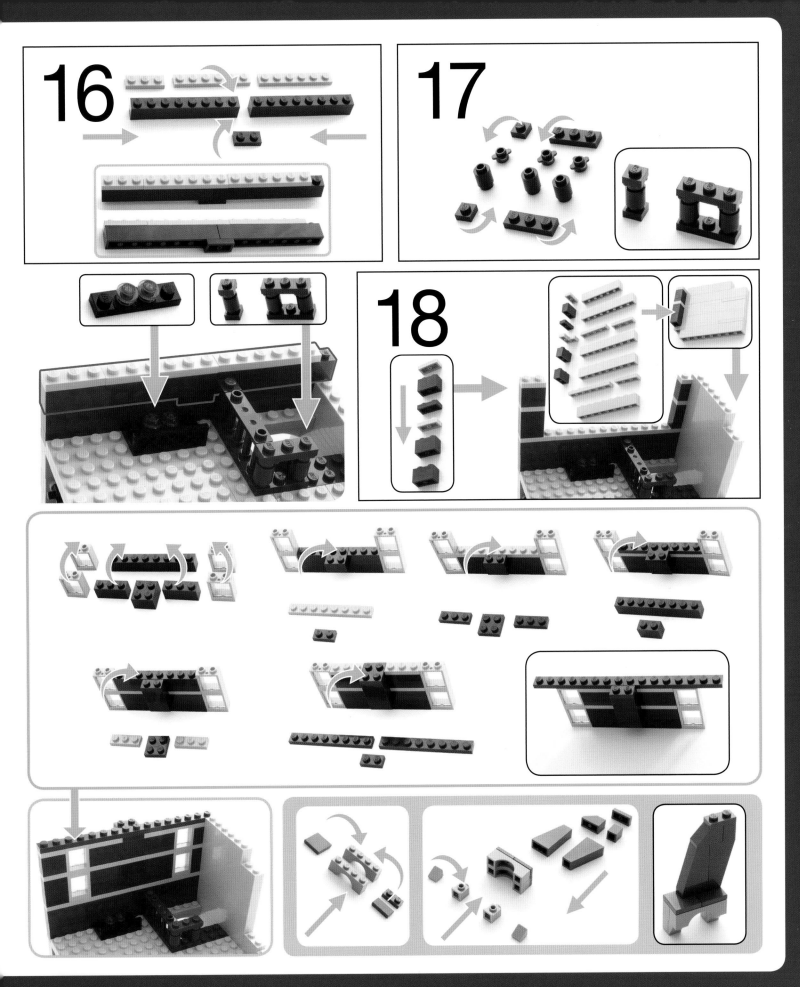

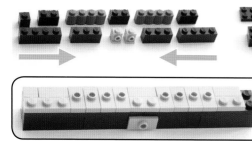

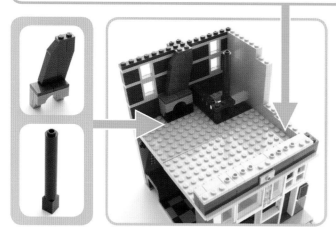

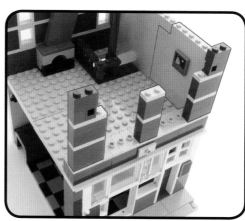

19

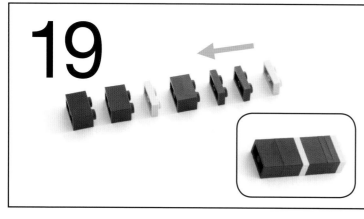

20

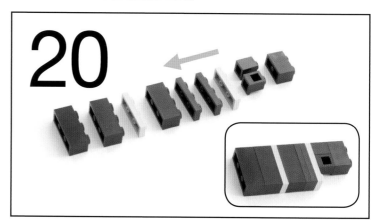

21

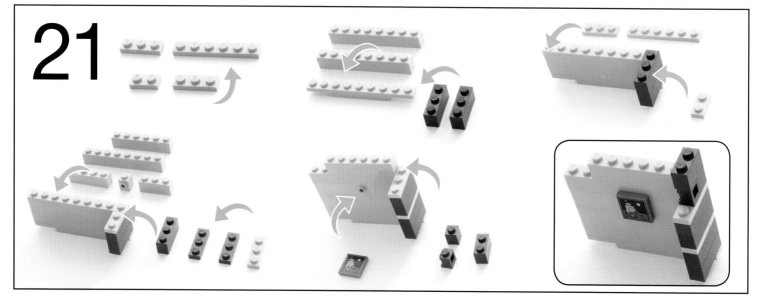

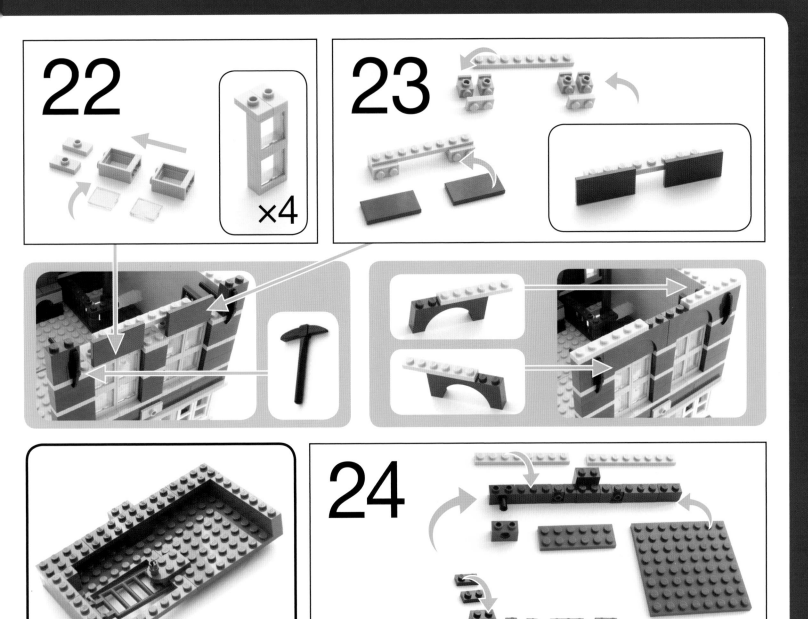

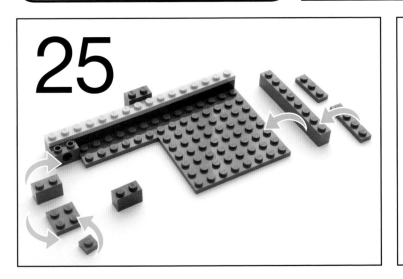

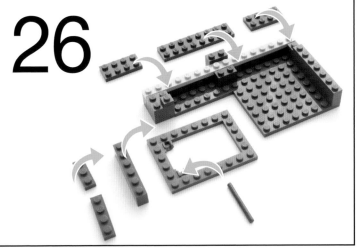

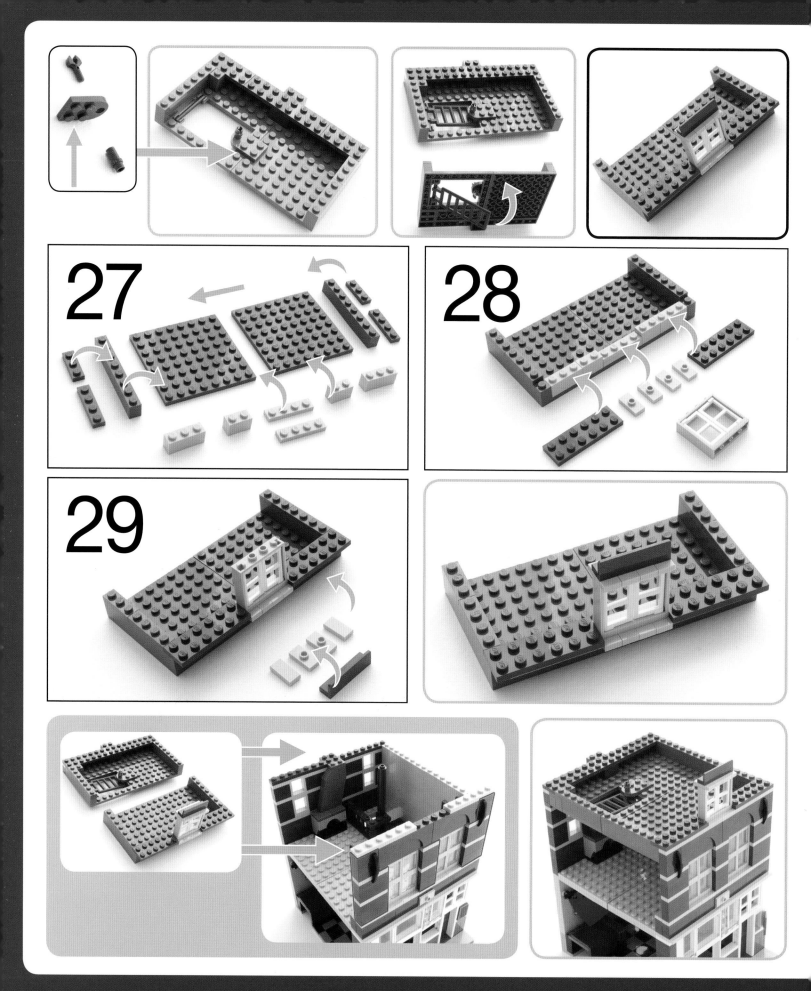

27

28

29

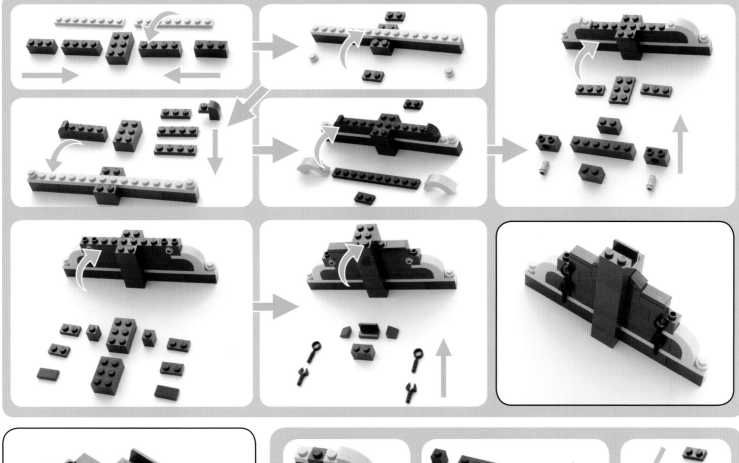

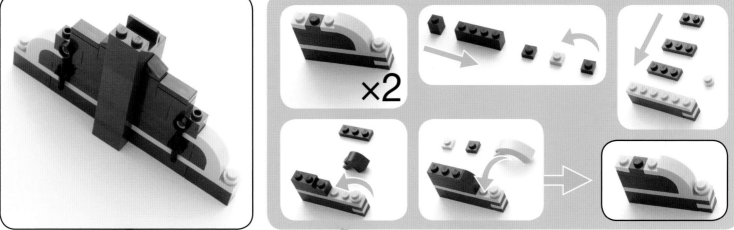

×2

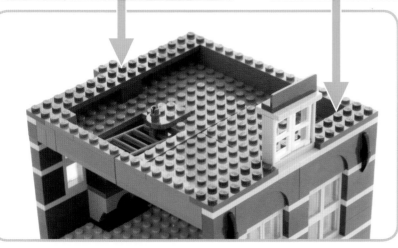

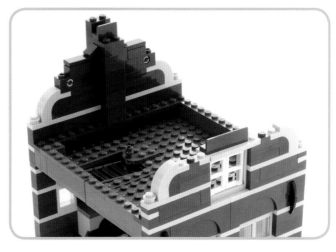

30

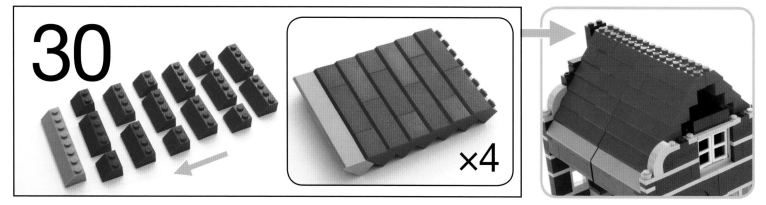

×4

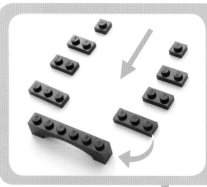

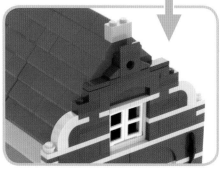

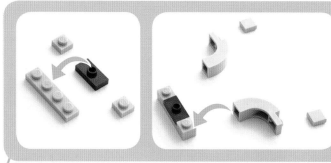

×2

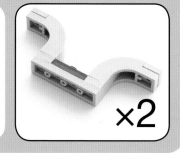

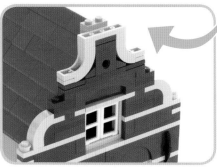

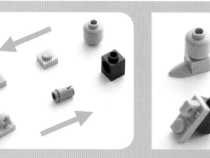

×4

31

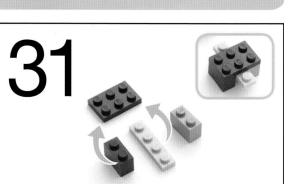

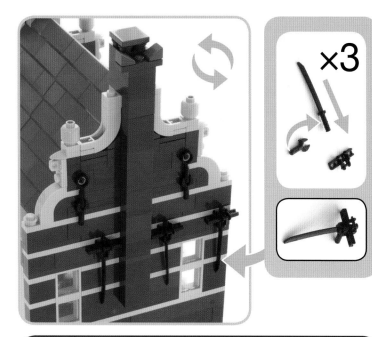

×3

Patrick's LEGO buildings are brilliant! He told me that he likes to base his models on real buildings. Before he builds, he does a lot of research and likes to learn about the building's history so that he can capture its character. Using elements in unconventional ways allows for lots of detail, too. Now I'm wondering what My Idea Lab might look like with some cool Dutch spires!

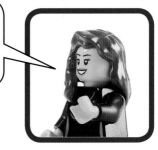

THERE, THAT'S MUCH BETTER!

WELL, FUNNY YOU SHOULD ASK, MEGS. HERE'S THE BUST FROM THE ENTRY TO THE DORDRECHT GATE.

IT'S GORGEOUS! YOU HAVE A GREAT PLACE TO LIVE AND WORK FOR SURE, PATRICK! HAVE YOU BUILT ANYTHING ELSE?

Statue

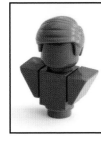

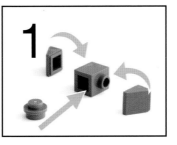

1

2

Groothoofdspoort: Dordrecht City Gate

Dutch Coach

River Boat

Building Tip
Adding various means of transport will bring your city to life. Just keep in mind what historical period you're building in so you can stay true to it.

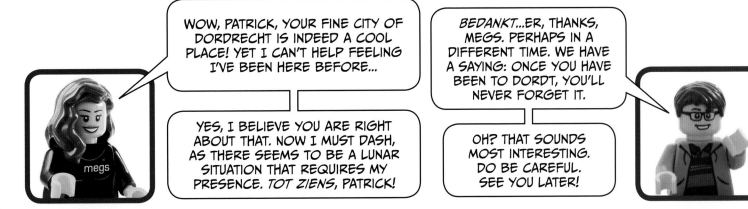

WOW, PATRICK, YOUR FINE CITY OF DORDRECHT IS INDEED A COOL PLACE! YET I CAN'T HELP FEELING I'VE BEEN HERE BEFORE...

YES, I BELIEVE YOU ARE RIGHT ABOUT THAT. NOW I MUST DASH, AS THERE SEEMS TO BE A LUNAR SITUATION THAT REQUIRES MY PRESENCE. *TOT ZIENS*, PATRICK!

BEDANKT...ER, THANKS, MEGS. PERHAPS IN A DIFFERENT TIME. WE HAVE A SAYING: ONCE YOU HAVE BEEN TO DORDT, YOU'LL NEVER FORGET IT.

OH? THAT SOUNDS MOST INTERESTING. DO BE CAREFUL. SEE YOU LATER!

In Deep Space

Peter Reid

Nickname: Legoloverman

Profession: Postman

Nationality: British

Website: *www.flickr.com/photos/legoloverman/*

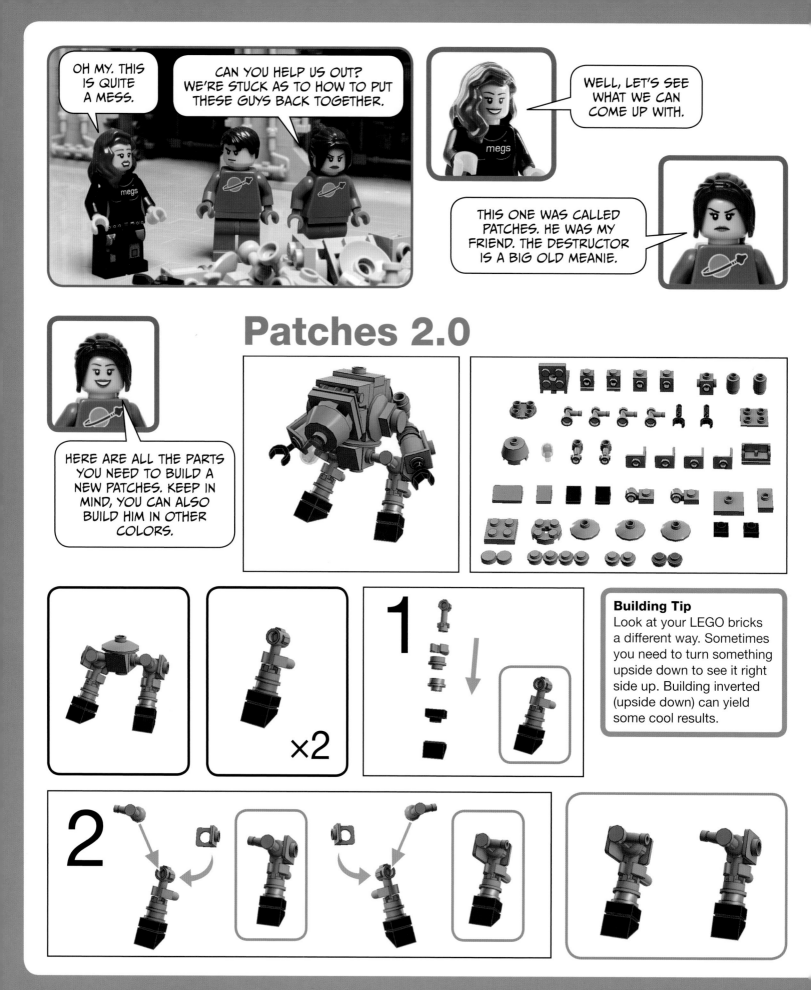

Patches 2.0

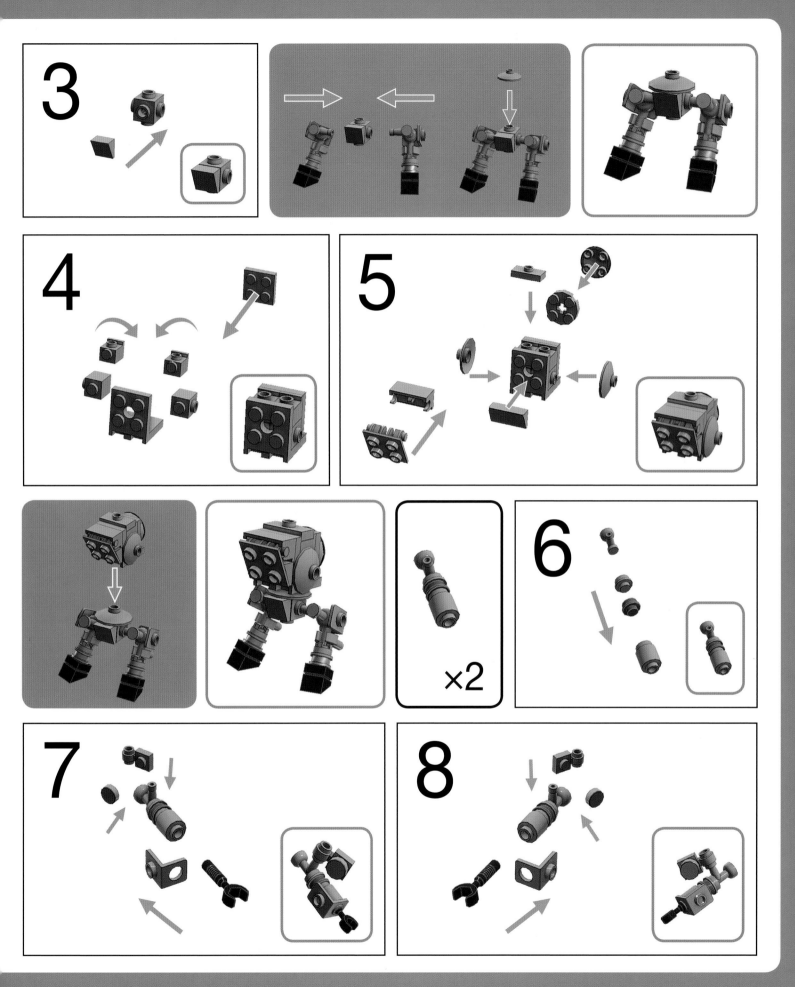

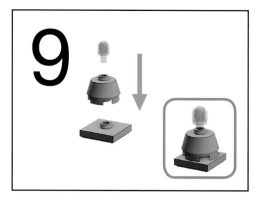

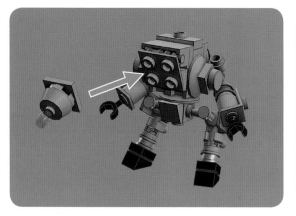

Building Tip
A few key color changes can alter the character of your robot. Using different colors is a nice way to visually communicate a robot's job; for example, you could use blue for a medical one. Alternatively, using a unified color scheme for several robots is a nice technique in a layout.

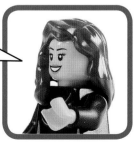

Trouble in Eden

Birgitte Jonsgard

Nickname: birgburg

Profession: Science teacher

Nationality: Norwegian

Website: *www.flickr.com/people/birgburg/*

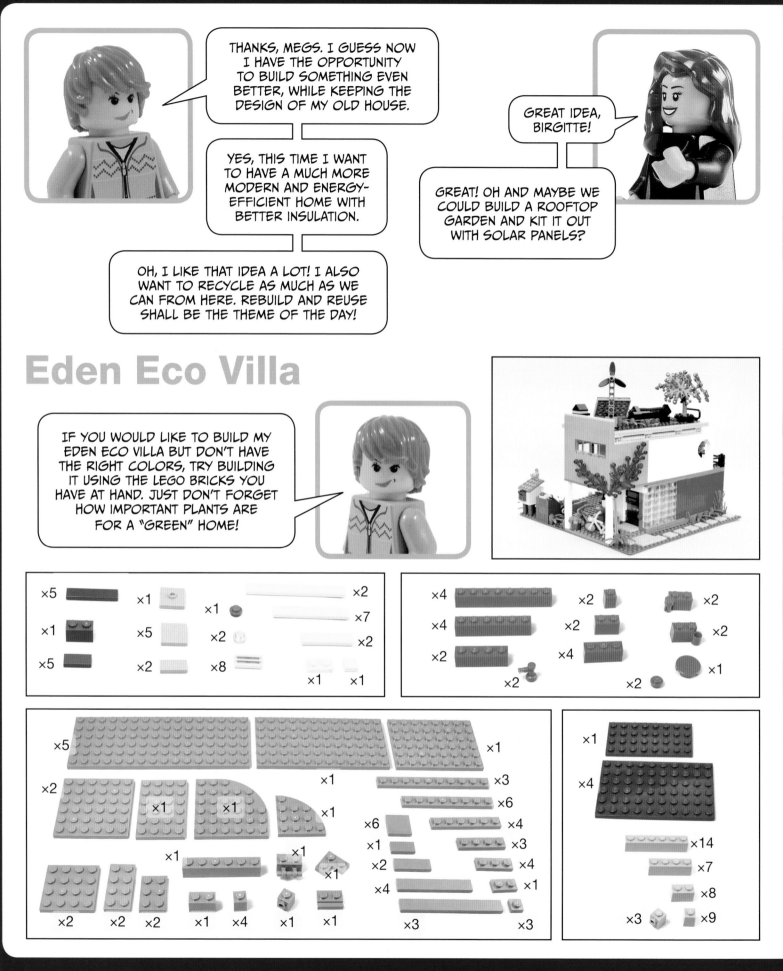

Eden Eco Villa

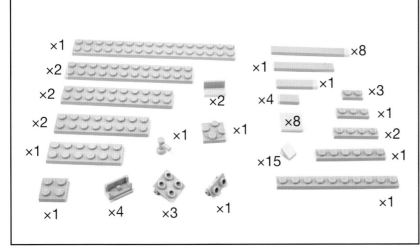

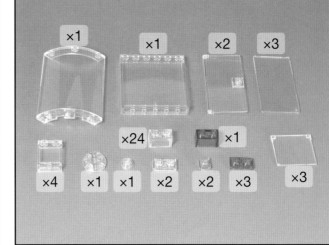

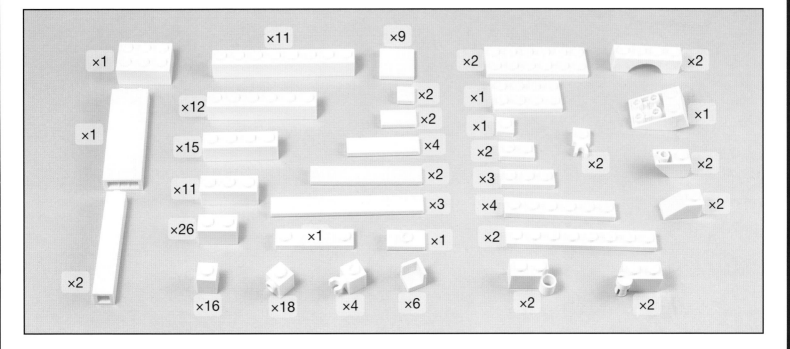

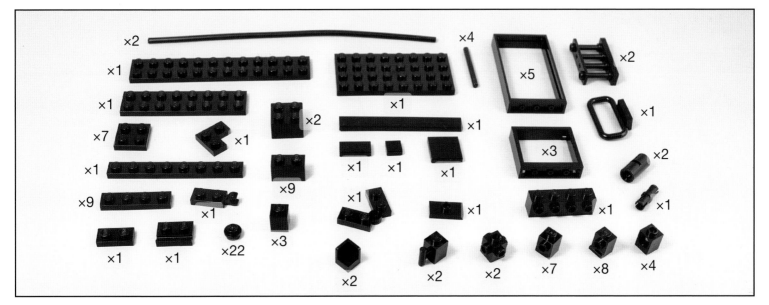

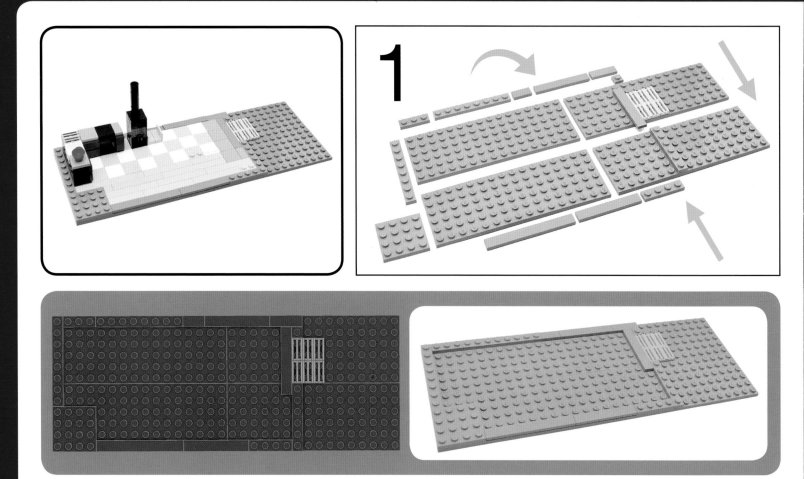

1

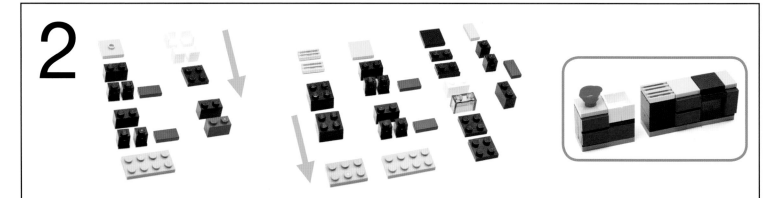

2

3

Building Tip
It doesn't take a lot of LEGO bricks to make some neat cabinets or a cozy fireplace, and these kinds of details will really bring your LEGO home to life.

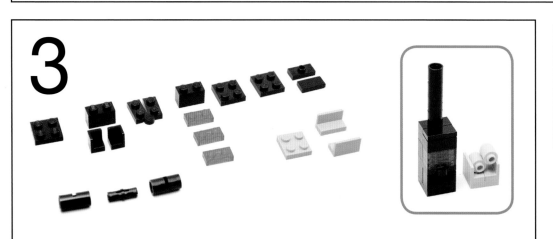

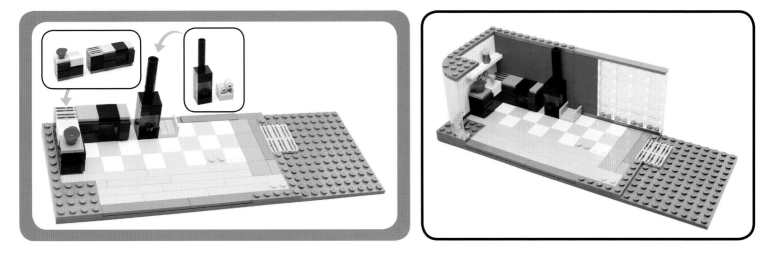

4

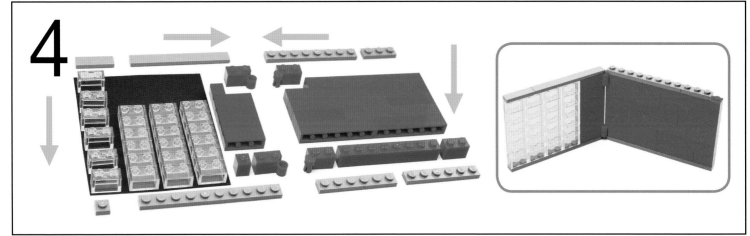

5

6

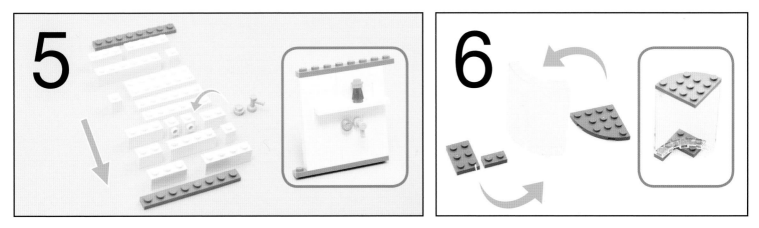

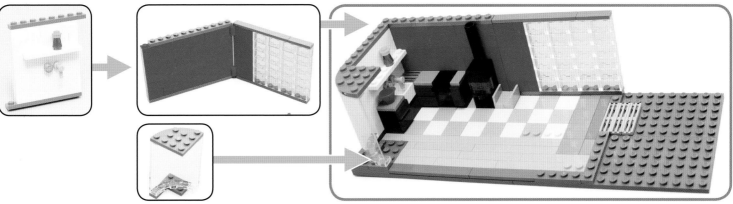

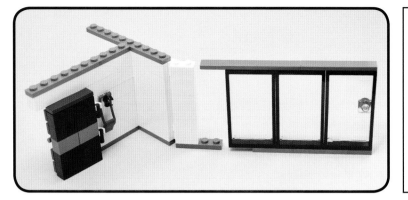

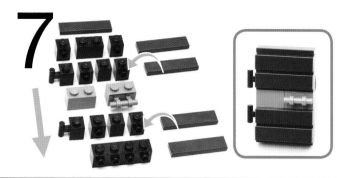

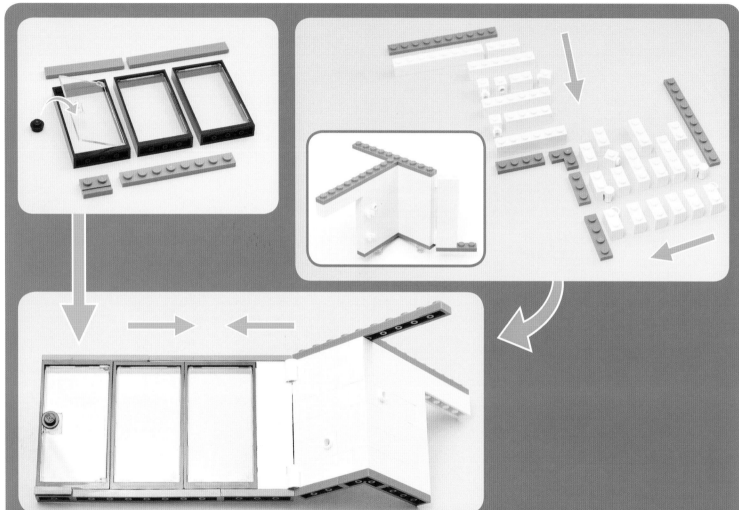

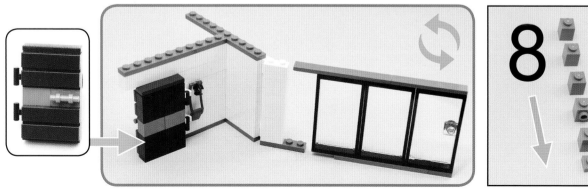

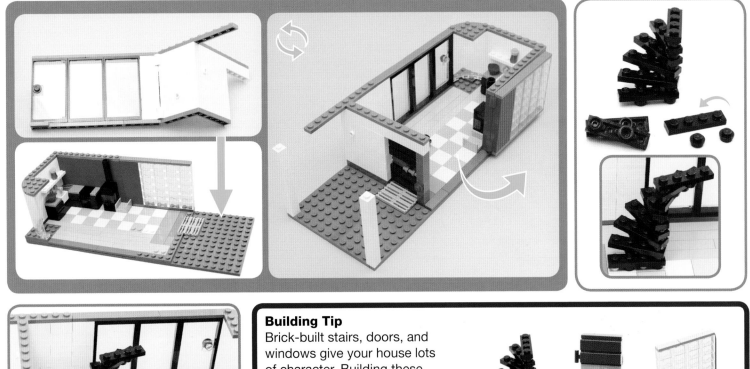

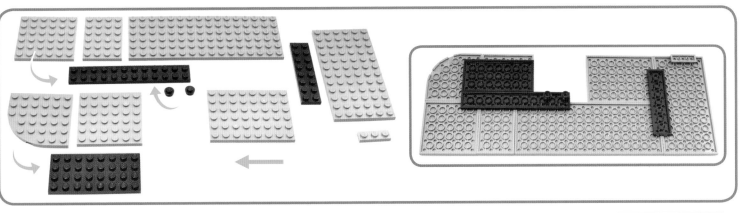

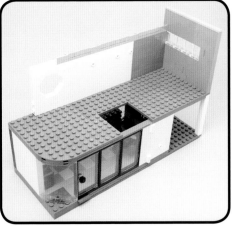

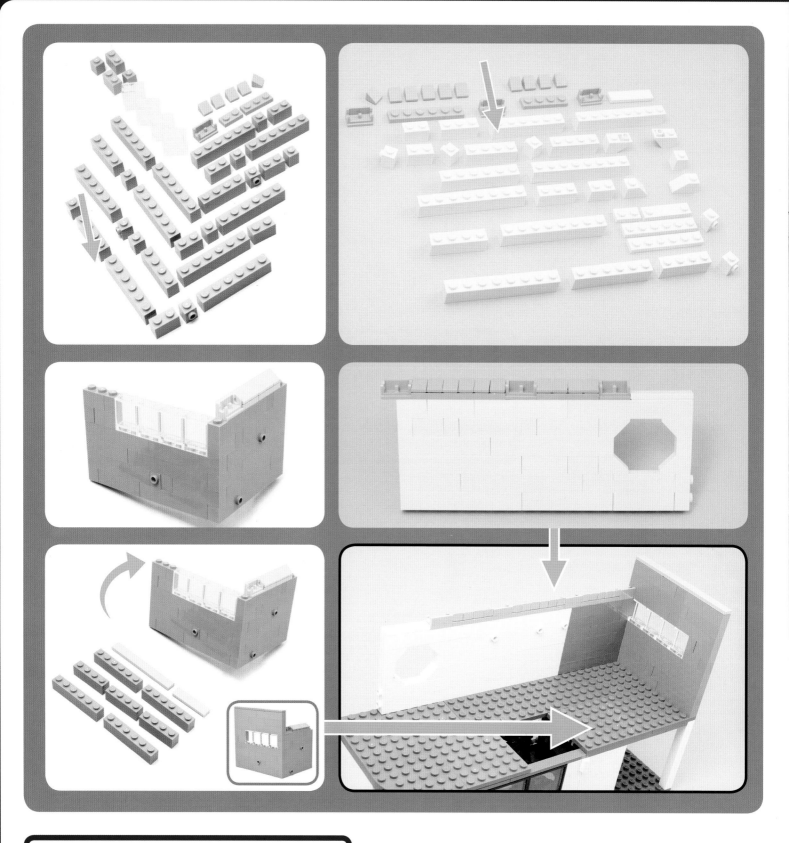

Building Tip
Don't forget to think about how to access your house. Adding 1×1 or 1×2 wedges with a rocker plate hinge will create a roof that opens, allowing for more playability.

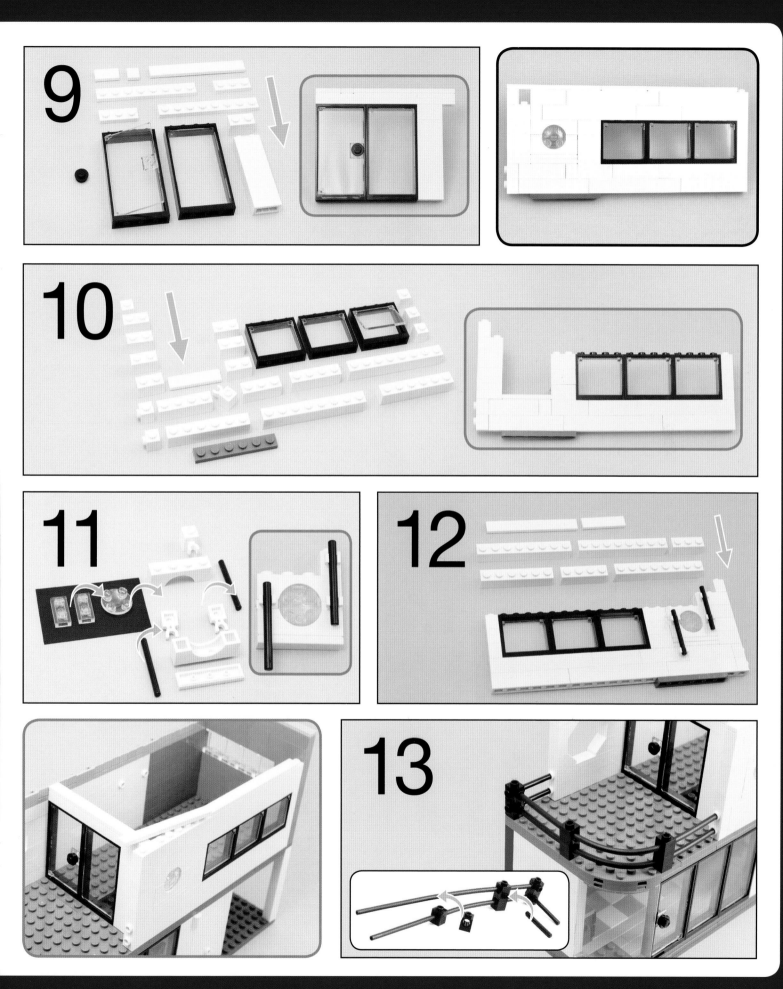

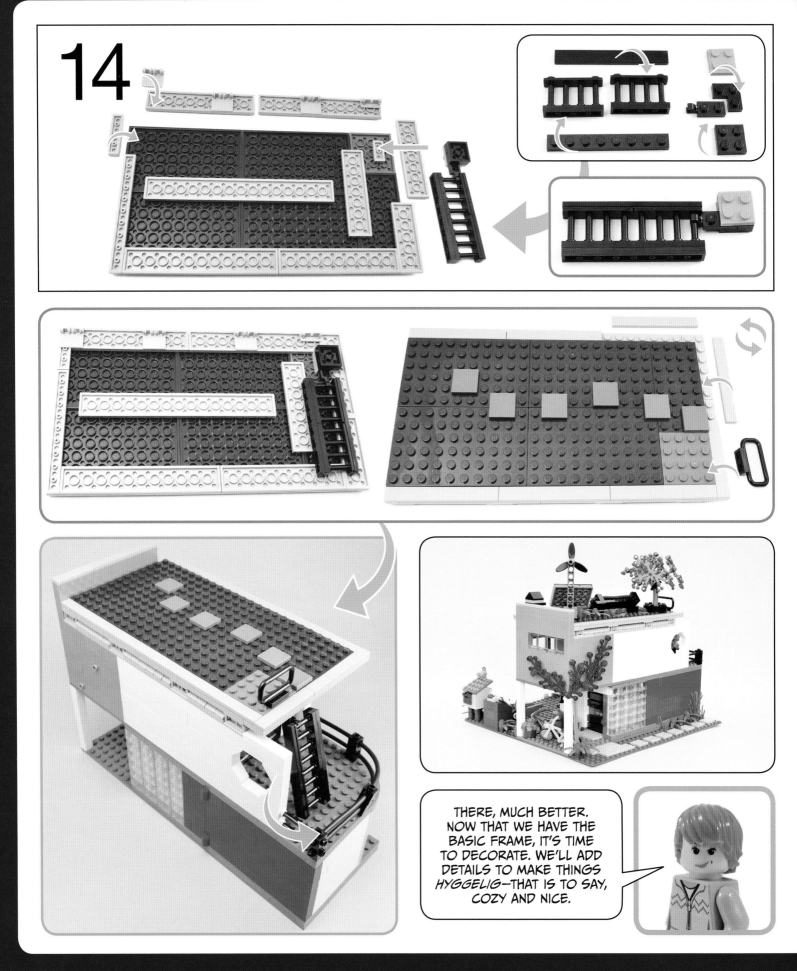

THERE, MUCH BETTER. NOW THAT WE HAVE THE BASIC FRAME, IT'S TIME TO DECORATE. WE'LL ADD DETAILS TO MAKE THINGS *HYGGELIG*—THAT IS TO SAY, COZY AND NICE.

Design Details with Birgitte

HERE ARE SOME HANDY TIPS FOR PLANNING YOUR INTERIORS. REMEMBER YOU CAN MAKE YOUR LIVING SPACE PRACTICAL AND INTERESTING; IT DOES NOT HAVE TO BE BORING. FOR INSTANCE, WHEN DESIGNING A ROOM THINK ABOUT BOTH SIDES OF THE WALL AND THEIR FUNCTIONS. HERE, ONE SIDE IS FOR THE BATHROOM AND THE OTHER SIDE HAS A WARDROBE FOR THE BEDROOM.

REMEMBER TO PLACE BRICKS WITH STUDS ON THE SIDE WHERE YOU WANT TO ATTACH THINGS—LIKE PICTURES, TAPS, AND CLIMBING PLANTS—TO THE WALLS. IT IS A GOOD IDEA TO PLAN WHERE TO PUT THEM BEFOREHAND!

Classic Lamp

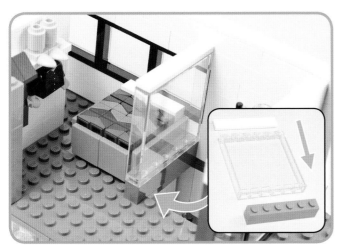

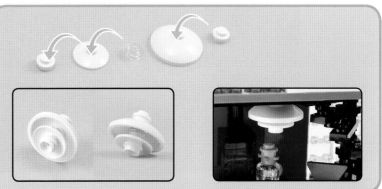

Vintage ANT7 Chairs

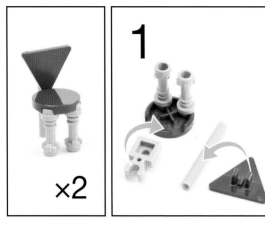

×2

1
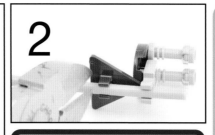

2
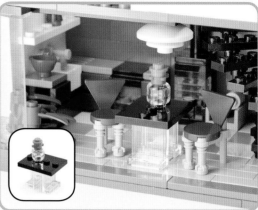

Building Tip
Be sure to get help from an older person when making your own length of tubing!

Patio Furniture

1
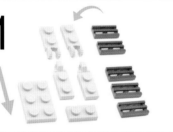

Building Tip
Think about the function of your building's space and build furnishings to complement it. Plants can create a relaxing space.

2

Cherry Tree

1

2
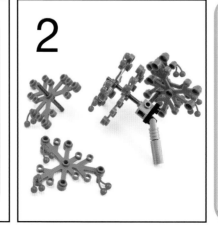

Exterior Foliage

Solar Panel

Hot Water Heater

Wind Turbine

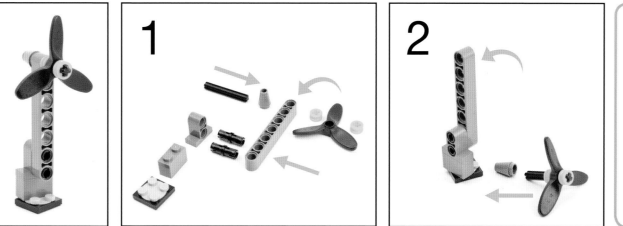

1

2

Compost Bin

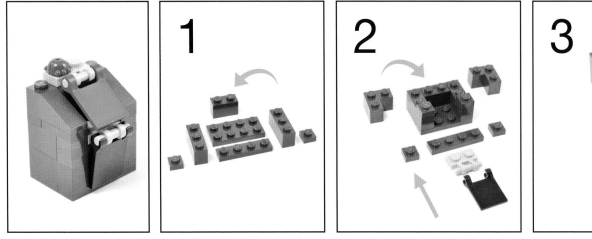

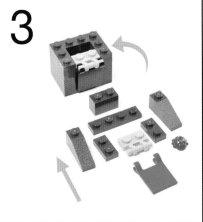

Beehive

Chicken Coop

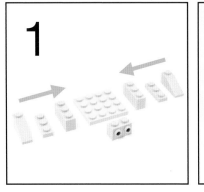

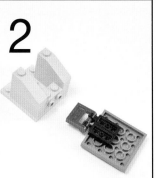

WONDERFUL! I AM SO HAPPY WITH MY NEW HOME, THANK YOU FOR YOUR HELP, MEGS!

YOU ARE MOST WELCOME, BIRGITTE. YOUR ROOFTOP GARDEN IS REALLY NICE, AND I LIKE YOUR BEEHIVE, TOO.

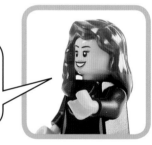

YES, I NEED BEES TO POLLINATE MY PLANTS IF I WANT A GOOD CROP OF CHERRIES THIS YEAR! ALSO, MY WIND TURBINE AND SOLAR PANELS WILL GENERATE ENOUGH ELECTRICITY FOR MY HOME, AND THE SUN WILL HEAT MY BLACK WATER TANK SO I CAN HAVE HEAT AND HOT WATER.

BUILDING JOURNAL

Birgitte's Eden Eco Villa is brilliant! She has really put a lot of thought into planning a space that works for her lifestyle. Her choice of white with muted "sand" tones creates a clean look and a calm and relaxing space. At the same time, adding a splash of red to one of the walls helps to warm it up.

Building in so much detail gives a sense of realism. She told me that she pays attention to the things that surround her, like tiles, weeds, doormats, and trees. Attention to all of these details brings everything together. Her new pad is truly Zen. My Thinking Tower could use some of her touches.

I CAN USE MY CLIPPINGS FROM THE GARDEN IN MY COMPOST BIN. WITHIN A FEW MONTHS, BACTERIA AND EARTHWORMS WILL TURN IT INTO A NICE MULCH SO I CAN HAVE GOOD SOIL FOR MY GARDEN.

ABSOLUTELY, AND WITH THE NEW INSULATION, YOU'LL BE WARM AND SNUG IN THE WINTER AND COOL IN THE SUMMER.

THAT IS VERY TRUE, MEGS. LET'S GO RELAX ON THE LAWN AND HAVE SOME APPLES AND CHERRIES.

IT IS VERY IMPORTANT TO UNWIND—FOR THE BODY AND THE MIND.

AAAHHH, THIS IS INDEED LOVELY! I MUST REMEMBER HOW IMPORTANT IT IS TO TAKE A BREAK EVERY NOW AND AGAIN.

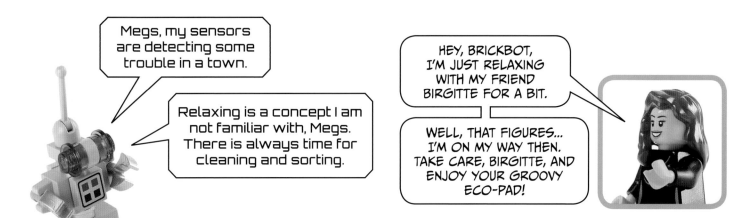

Megs, my sensors are detecting some trouble in a town.

Relaxing is a concept I am not familiar with, Megs. There is always time for cleaning and sorting.

HEY, BRICKBOT, I'M JUST RELAXING WITH MY FRIEND BIRGITTE FOR A BIT.

WELL, THAT FIGURES... I'M ON MY WAY THEN. TAKE CARE, BIRGITTE, AND ENJOY YOUR GROOVY ECO-PAD!

A LEGO Town Revisited

Craig Mandeville

Nickname: Solitary Dark

Profession: Aircraft Parts Manager

Nationality: British

Website: *www.flickr.com/photos/36416029@N06/*

HMMM...THAT SOUNDS LIKE THE BAD-BOTS. CAN YOU SHOW ME THE WAY TO THE TOWN PLEASE? I NEED TO CATCH THOSE BOTS!

OF COURSE! LET'S JUST TAKE THE TRAM BACK TO TOWN FROM HERE.

THERE WE ARE, CENTRAL STATION AND RIGHT ON THE DOT!

Building Tip
Building a bridge from lots of different colored and textured LEGO bricks gives your model a more realistic look. Plus, adding plants and trees adds an additional layer of texture to any LEGO city.

Arcata Deco Cinema

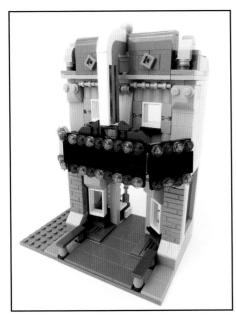

MY CINEMA IS A BIT TRICKY TO BUILD. YOU WILL NEED TO JUMP INTO YOUR DIRECTOR'S CHAIR AND PAY CLOSE ATTENTION TO THE FOOTPRINT. BE SURE TO ADD LOTS OF LIGHTS TO THE MARQUEE!

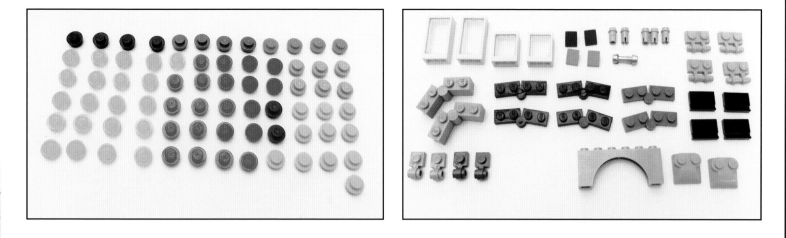

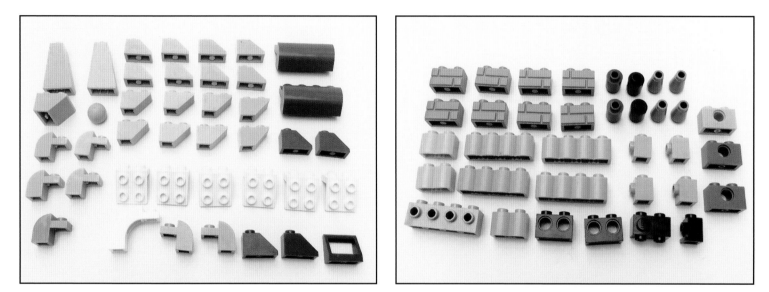

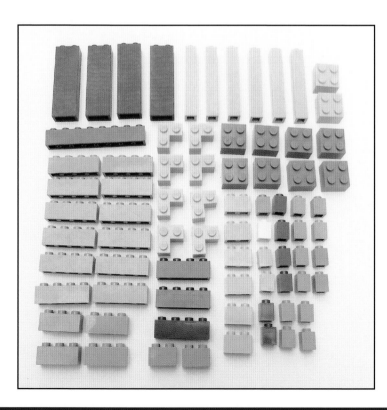

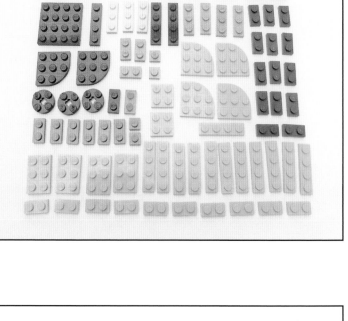

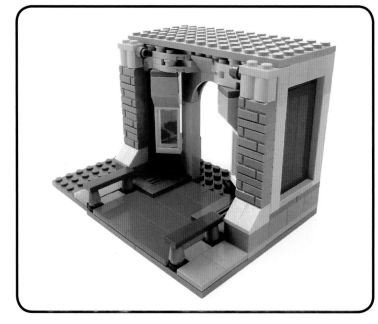

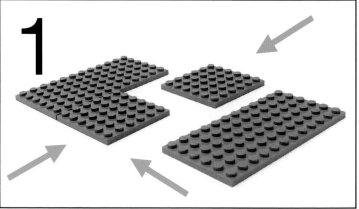

1

2

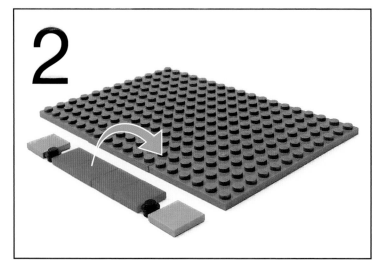

3

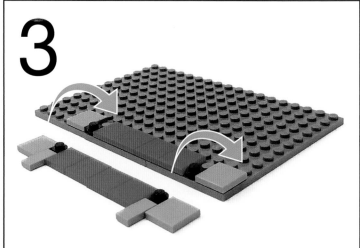

4

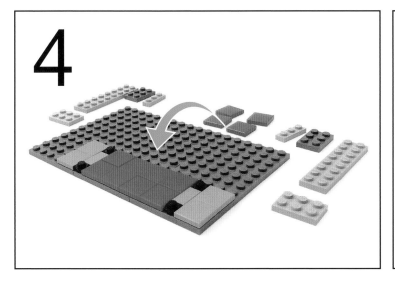

5

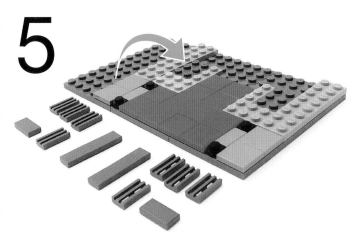

6

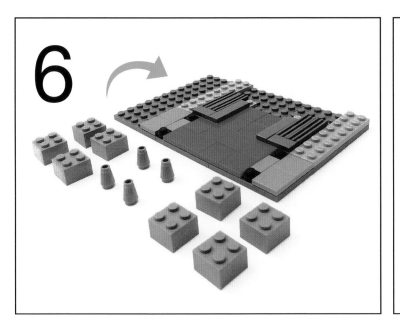

7

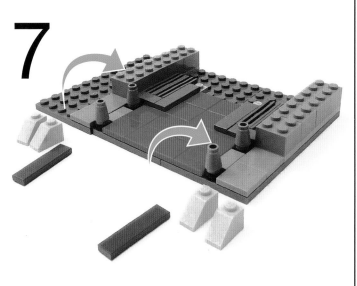

8

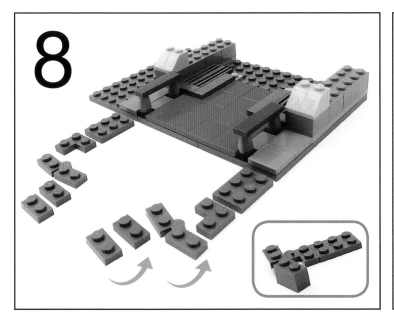

9

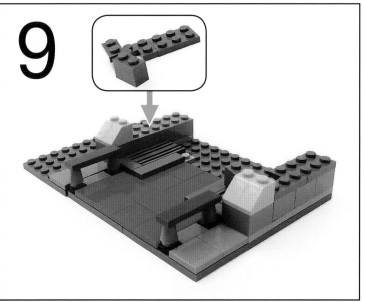

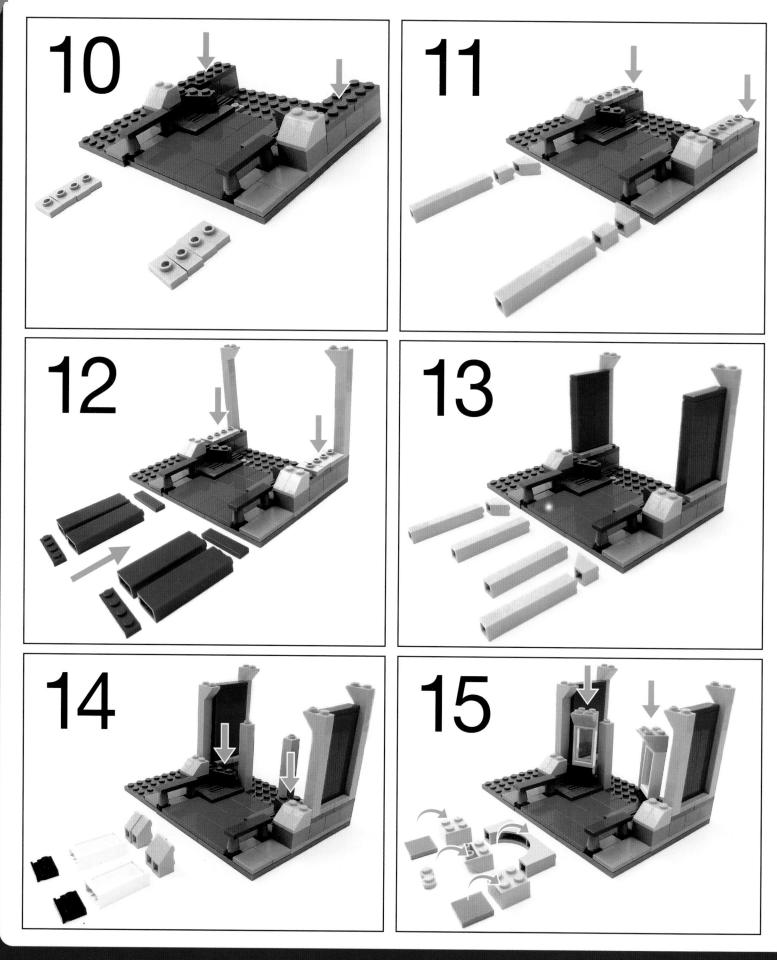

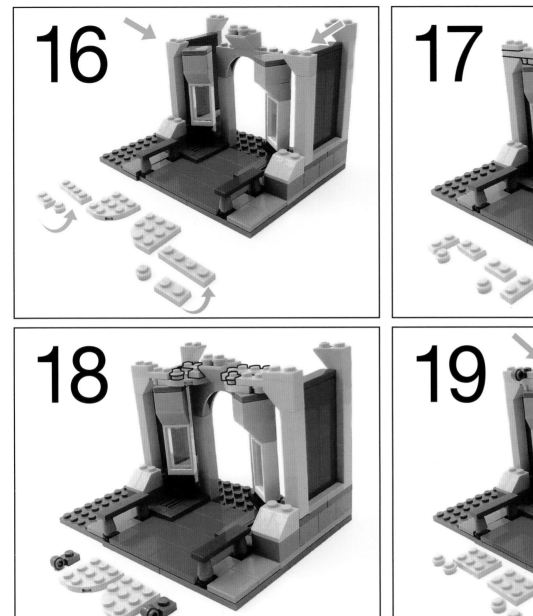

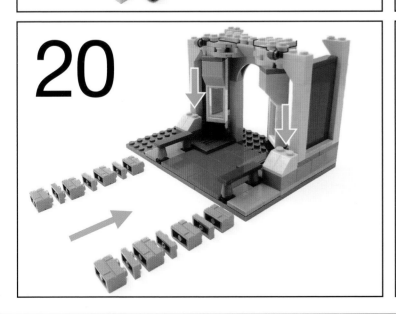

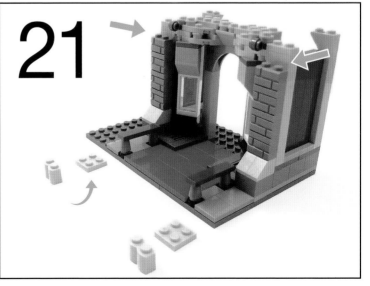

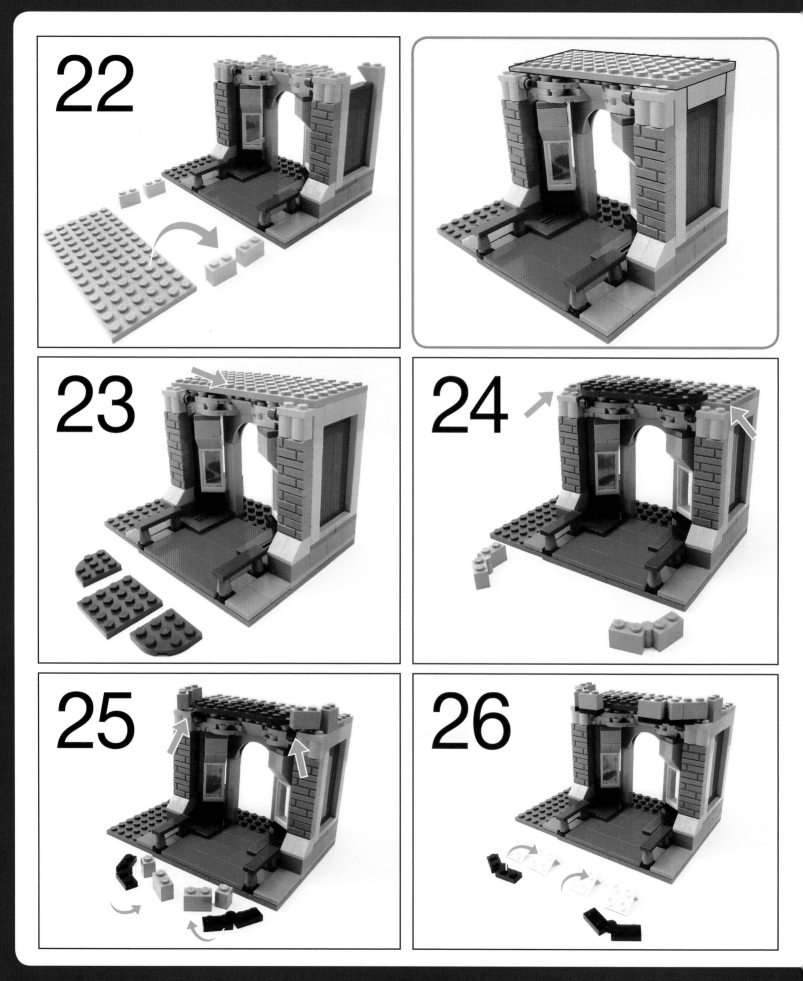

32

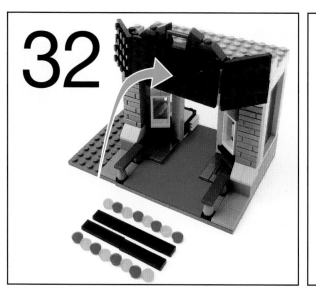

33

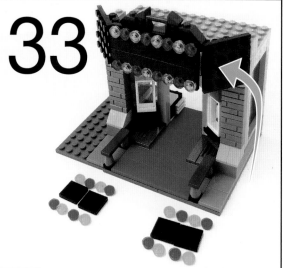

Building Tip
When designing a building, think about it's function and what assets can be added to create the right environment. For example, a movie theater like this one should have chairs, a screen, and a camera.

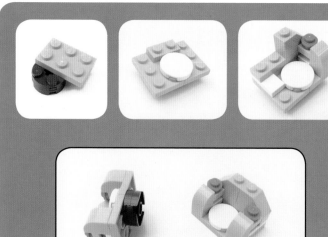

×2

34

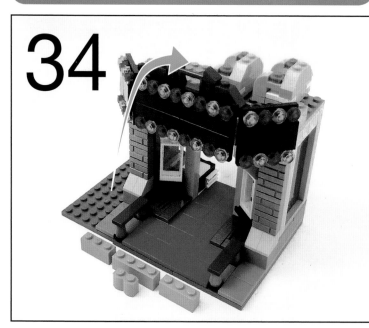

35

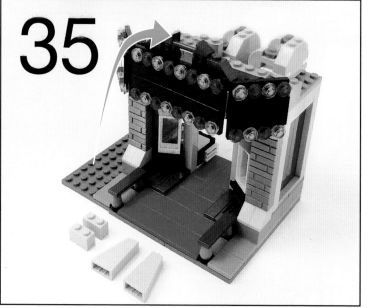

36

37

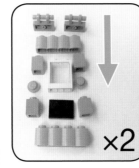

×2

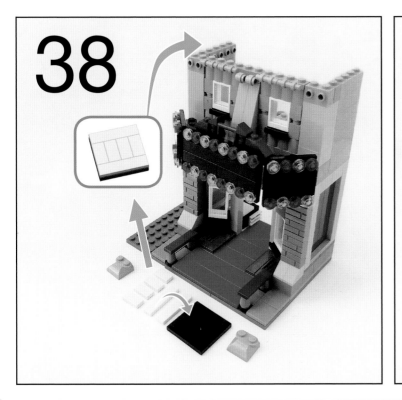

38

39

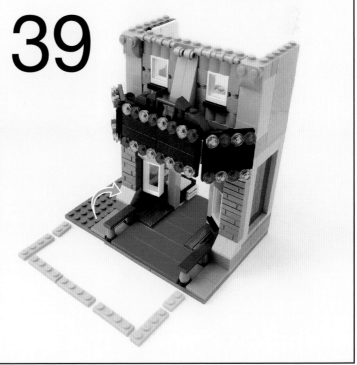

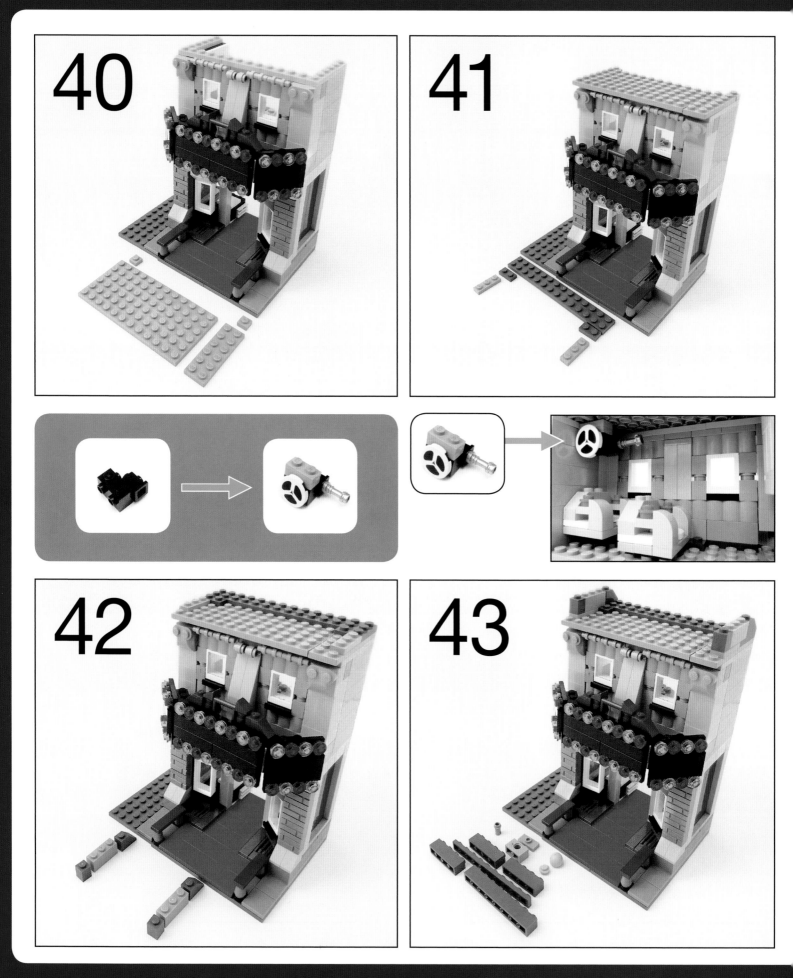

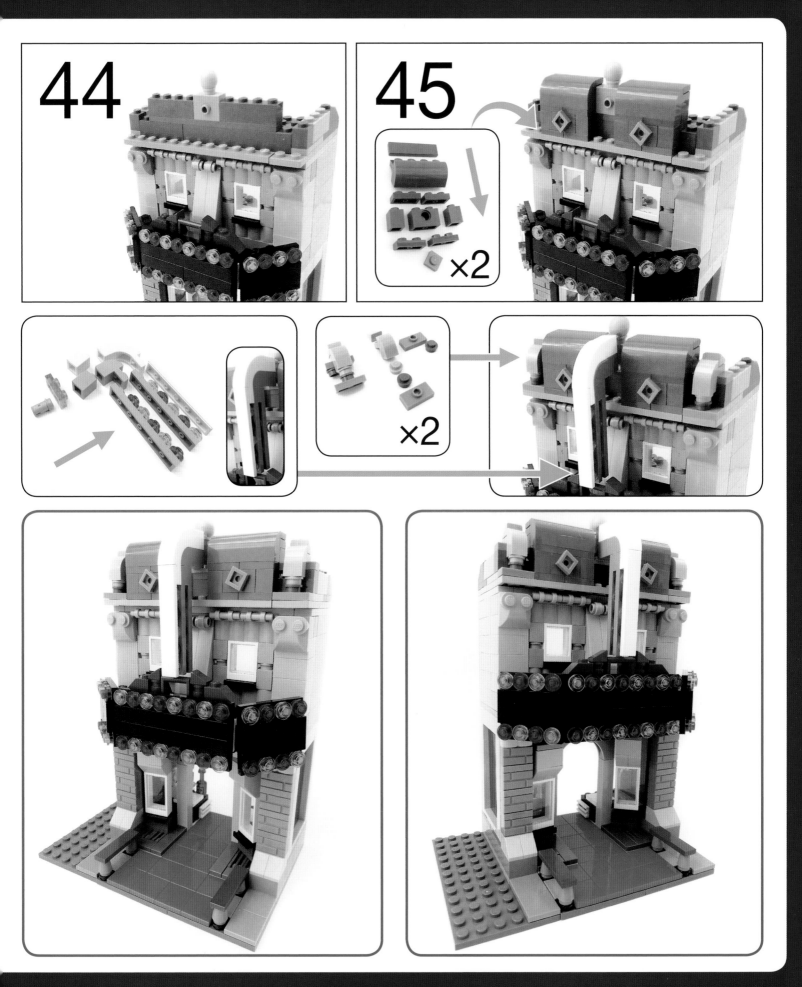

44

45

×2

×2

Popcorn Machine

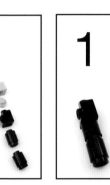

1

2

3

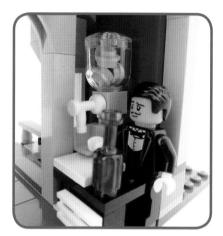

BUILDING JOURNAL

One of the great things about building a LEGO city is that you can build in many styles from many eras. Cities grow over the years, so each part can reflect the time when it was built. The oldest part of Craig's town is based on Victorian England. Trams like those he has built are still in use in parts of England today. He told me that he also loves building a wide variety of vehicles to go with his town. This helps to bring his LEGO town to life. Mixing different time periods seems like a great way to build a unique LEGO City.

BUILDING JOURNAL

Craig's models look brilliant! He has shown me that there is so much more to creating a LEGO town than just building houses or fire stations. There can be shops, parks, bridges, and so much more. He shared with me that the next big project for his town is a large bridge that vehicles can travel over and under. Changing the character of a bridge can be as simple as building in LEGO train tracks to make it a railway bridge.

Building Tip
When designing a building, choose the color scheme beforehand. For example, a mechanic's garage works well with shades of red and grey, while the magic shop in Craig's town is a more theatrical black, white, and purple. The coffee shop is tan, brown, and green. Different color schemes allow the buildings to be more distinctive when lined up against each other on a street.

Jukebox

ONE THING THAT BRINGS A LEGO TOWN TO LIFE IS THE DETAILS YOU CAN BUILD FOR YOUR TOWN'S INHABITANTS. HERE ARE A FEW EXAMPLES FOR YOU TO TRY.

1

2

3

4

5

6

7

Wheelchair

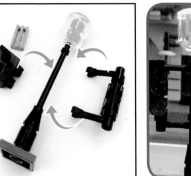 

Street Lamp

CREATING AN INTERESTING INTERIOR CAN ADD LOTS OF PLAY VALUE TO A BUILDING. A NEW BRANCH OF THE COFFEE SHOP HAS OPENED UP IN MY TOWN. MINIFIGURES CAN WORK BEHIND THE COUNTER, WHILE OTHERS ORDER THEIR MORNING COFFEE.

Coffee Shop 2.0

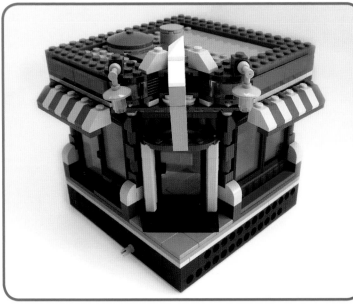 

LEGO Town Inspiration

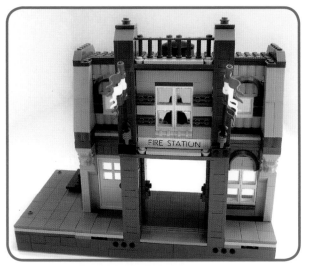

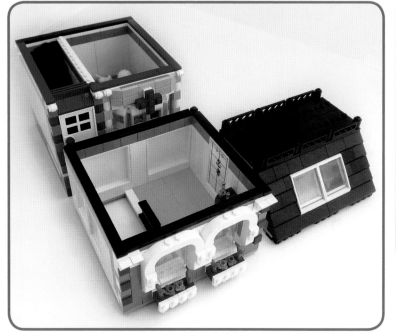

Building Tip
Placing LEGO plates in the corners and tiling the rest of each story's floor allows you to easily detach the stories and see inside, which means greater playability for your mini-figures!

LEGO Town Vehicles

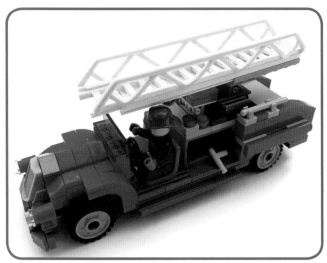

Building Tip
Designing a variety of interesting vehicles really brings a town to life. Varying the width, size, and scale of LEGO vehicles can give your town realistically busy streets.

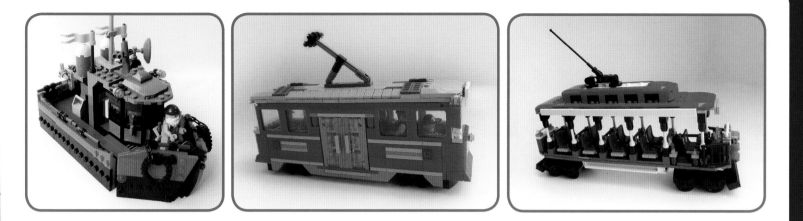

BUILDING JOURNAL

Craig has built some great vehicles. He told me that when you build a car or tram, you should think about the parts that will give your vehicle a personality or show what time period it comes from. For the orange trolley car, he added opening doors and big windows like the real cars that traveled the streets of Los Angeles in the 1930s. When building a version of a real-life vehicle, key in on the iconic details such as shape, size, bumpers, shape of lights, and windshield to help capture that specific vehicle's look.

MEGS, I JUST HAD A CALL FROM MY FRIEND ALAN. THE BAD-BOTS HAVE STRUCK AGAIN—ANOTHER ONE OF MY CREATIONS HAS BEEN DESTROYED! FOLLOW ME!

YES! LET'S REBUILD IT BETTER! WHILE YOU'VE HAD YOUR TRANSPORT-O-LUX, MEGS, I'VE BEEN LEARNING HOW TO FLY A PLANE.

YIKES! IT SOUNDS LIKE YOUR FRIEND ALAN'S PLANE HAS BEEN HIT BY THE DESTRUCTOR!

Alan's Airplane

BUILDING ALAN'S AIRPLANE WILL REQUIRE YOU TO PUT ON YOUR AIRCRAFT ENGINEER'S HAT. THERE IS A LOT OF MIRRORING OF THE PLANE'S HULL AND SIDES. IN ORDER TO TAKE TO THE SKIES, YOU WILL NEED TO STUDY THESE INSTRUCTIONS CLOSELY.

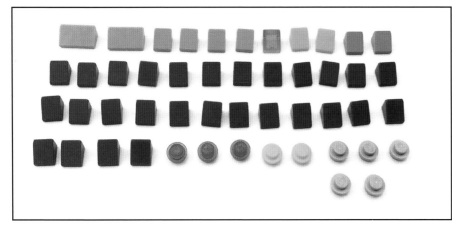

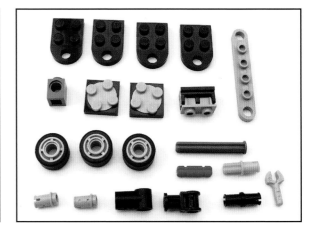

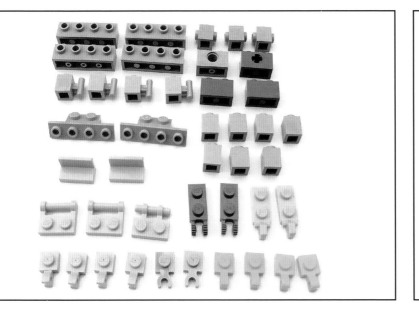

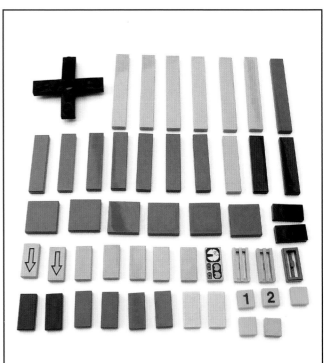

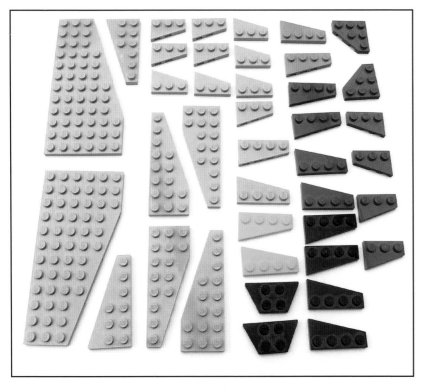

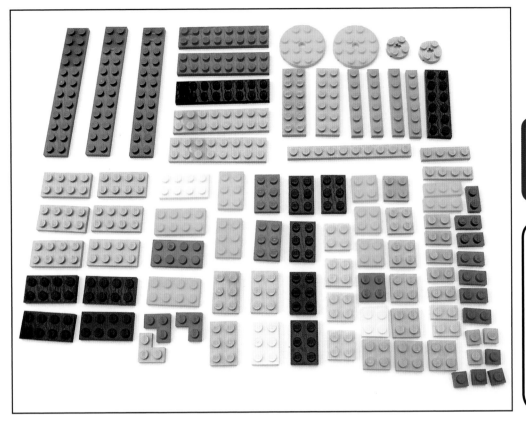

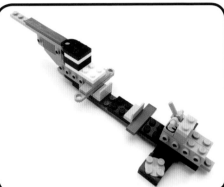

Building Tip
If you don't have these colors
of LEGO bricks, try building this
model in other colors.

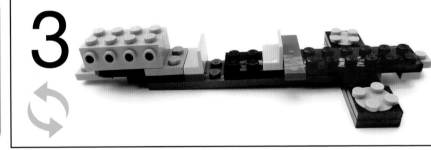

1

2

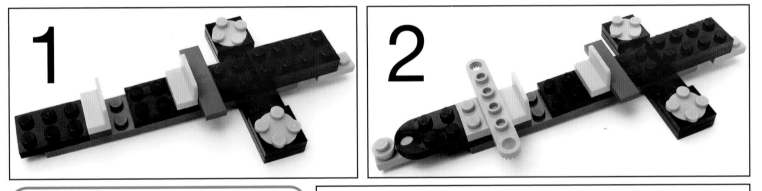

3

4

5

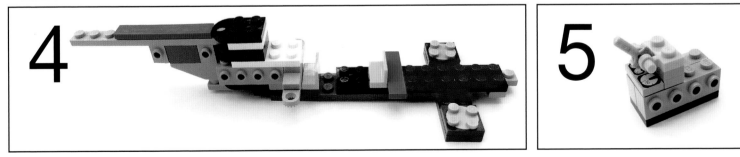

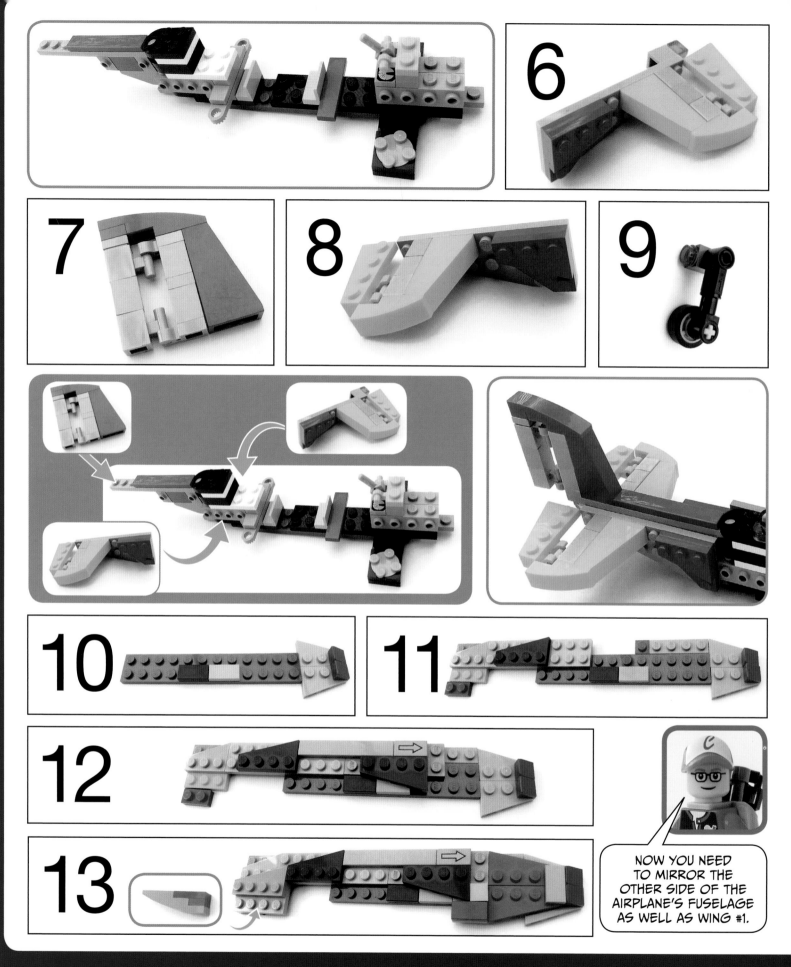

NOW YOU NEED TO MIRROR THE OTHER SIDE OF THE AIRPLANE'S FUSELAGE AS WELL AS WING #1.

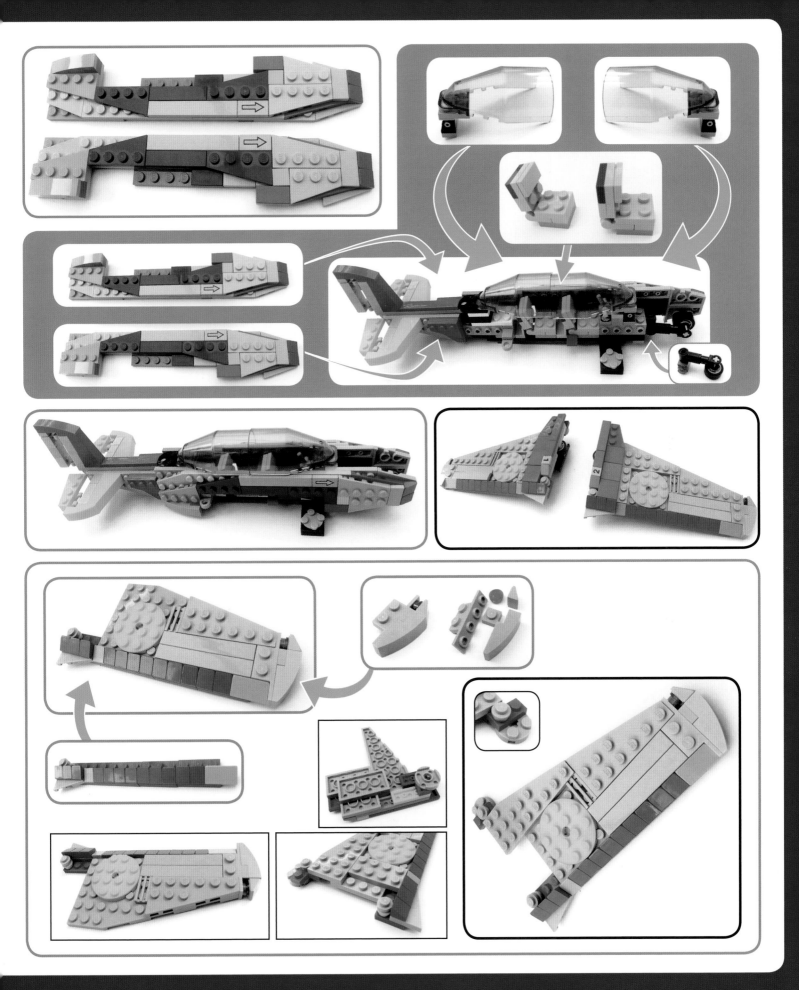

Steam Fair Fun!

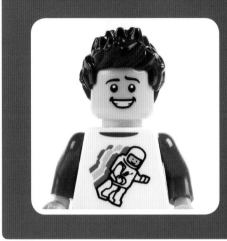

Jason Railton

Nickname: Joefish

Profession: IT Developer

Nationality: British

Website: www.flickr.com/photos/jjrailton/

GOOD IDEA, I WILL DRAFT UP SOME PLANS.

POOR DOBBIN! LET'S SORT THIS OUT AND REBUILD HIM.

DOBBIN MAY SEEM SMALL, BUT BUILDING HIM IS NOT AS EASY AS IT LOOKS. YOU'LL NEED SIDEWAYS BUILDING TECHNIQUES. FOCUS ON THE SPACING AND SUBMODULES. DON'T RACE THROUGH IT—SLOW AND STEADY IS BEST.

Dobbin the Shire Horse

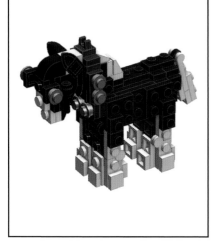

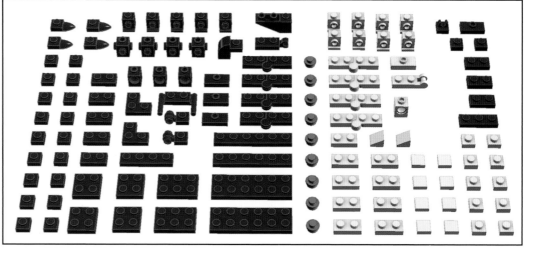

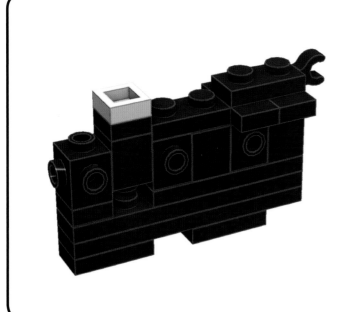

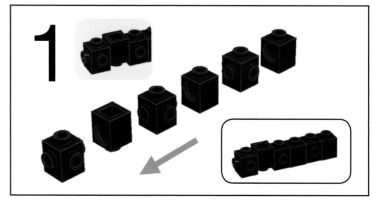

1

Building Tip

Many animals can be built using this core design with studs facing out on both sides: the bigger the animal, the wider the core. Make sure your legs are in the correct proportion, not too thin, too long, or too short for the creature you are building. A tail can be added on the clip end of the core, or if the animal has no tail, a 1×2 plate can replace the clip.

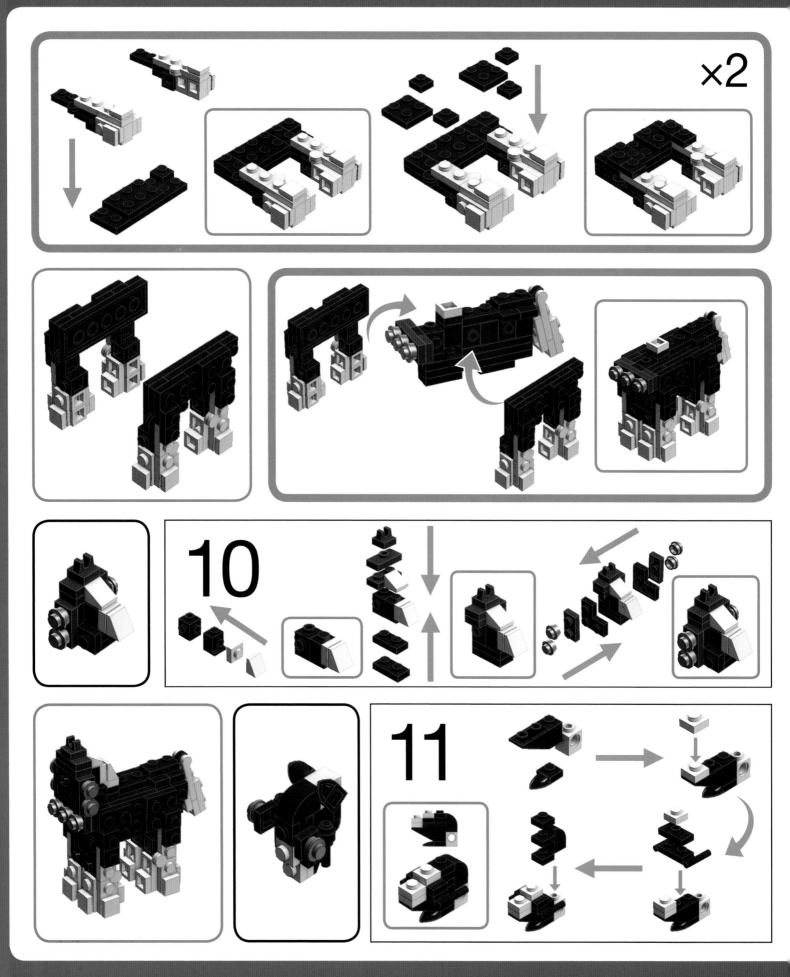

×2

10

11

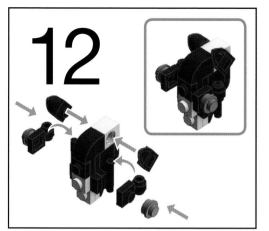

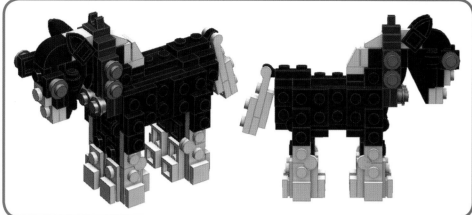

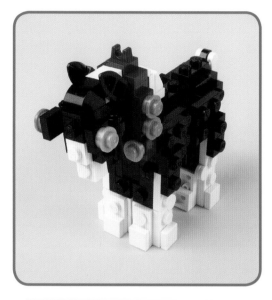

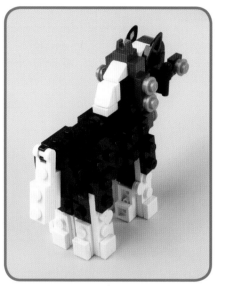

Building Tip
Study the anatomy of the animal that you are trying to build and sculpt the muscles in the right places using layers of plates.

BRILLIANT! DOBBIN IS ALL READY TO GET BACK TO WORK.

GRAB YOUR TINKERER'S HAT AND GET READY TO GET INTO GEARING. THE LADYBIRD WHIRL IS BUILT WITH A SMALL LEGO POWER FUNCTIONS MOTOR. WHILE THE MODEL IS FAIRLY STRAIGHTFORWARD, THE GEARING CAN BE TRICKY. I'VE BROKEN UP THE BUILD INTO SUBMODULES TO MAKE IT EASIER FOR YOU TO FOLLOW.

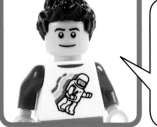

Ladybird Whirl

Base Module

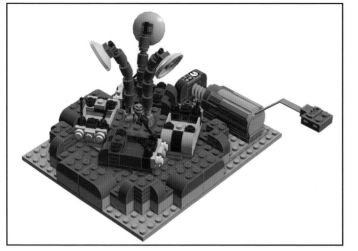

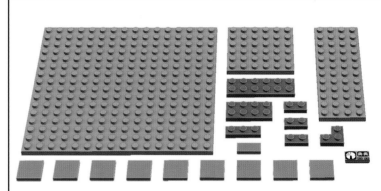

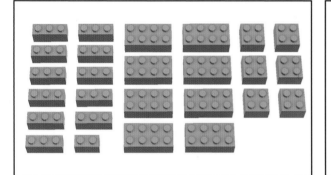

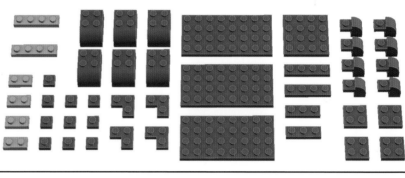

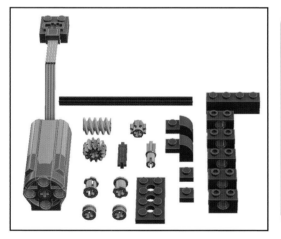

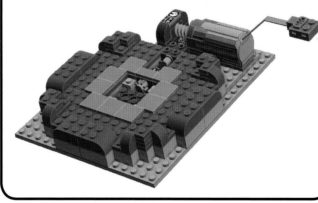

Building Tip
Designing a good solid base is very important for your ride.

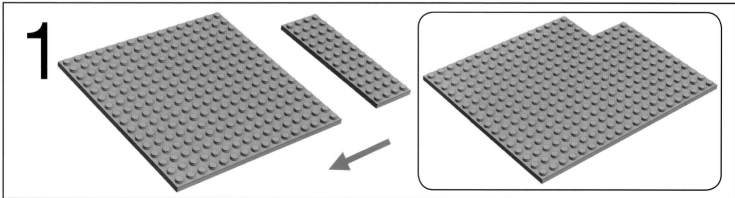

1

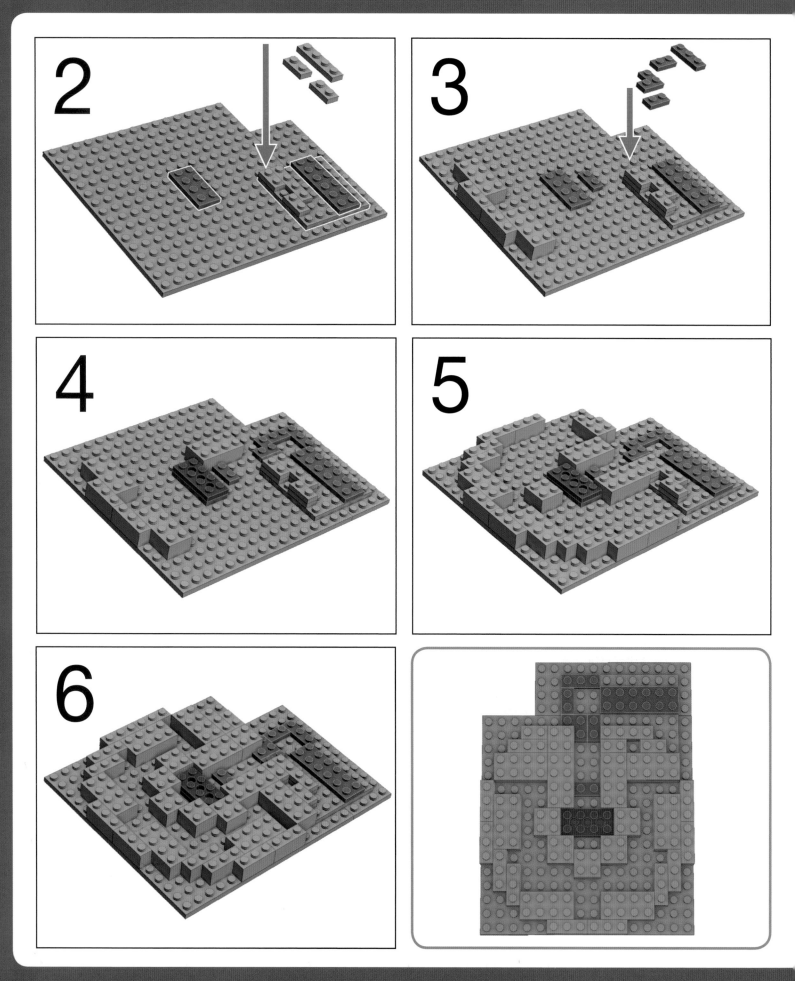

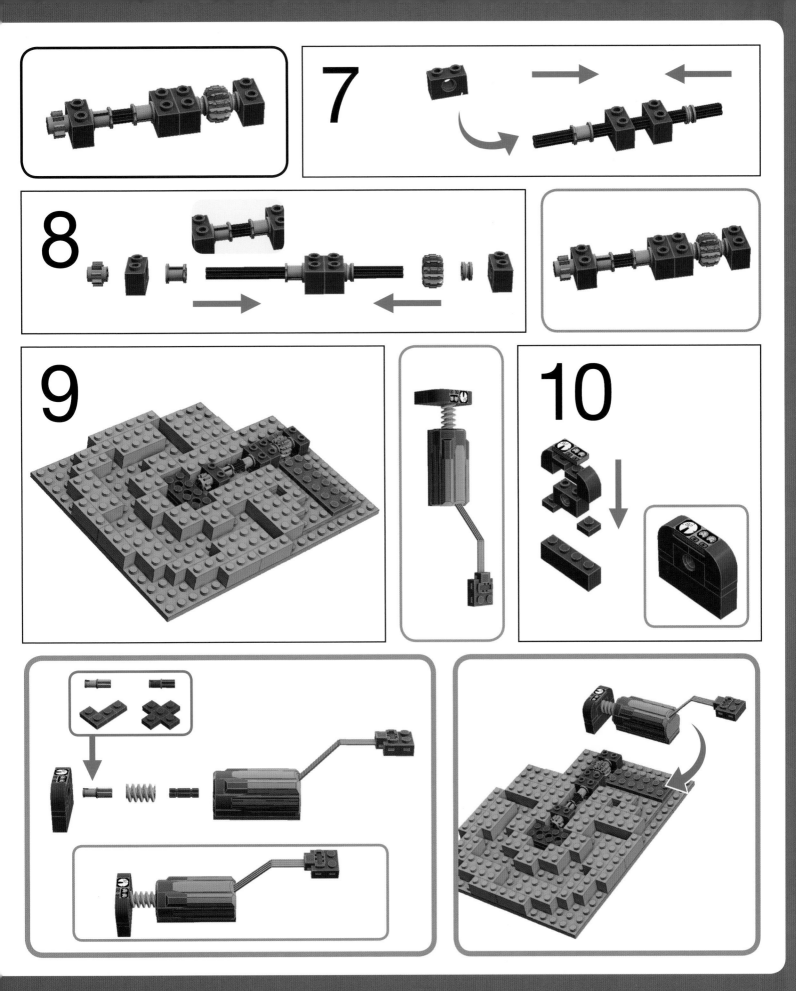

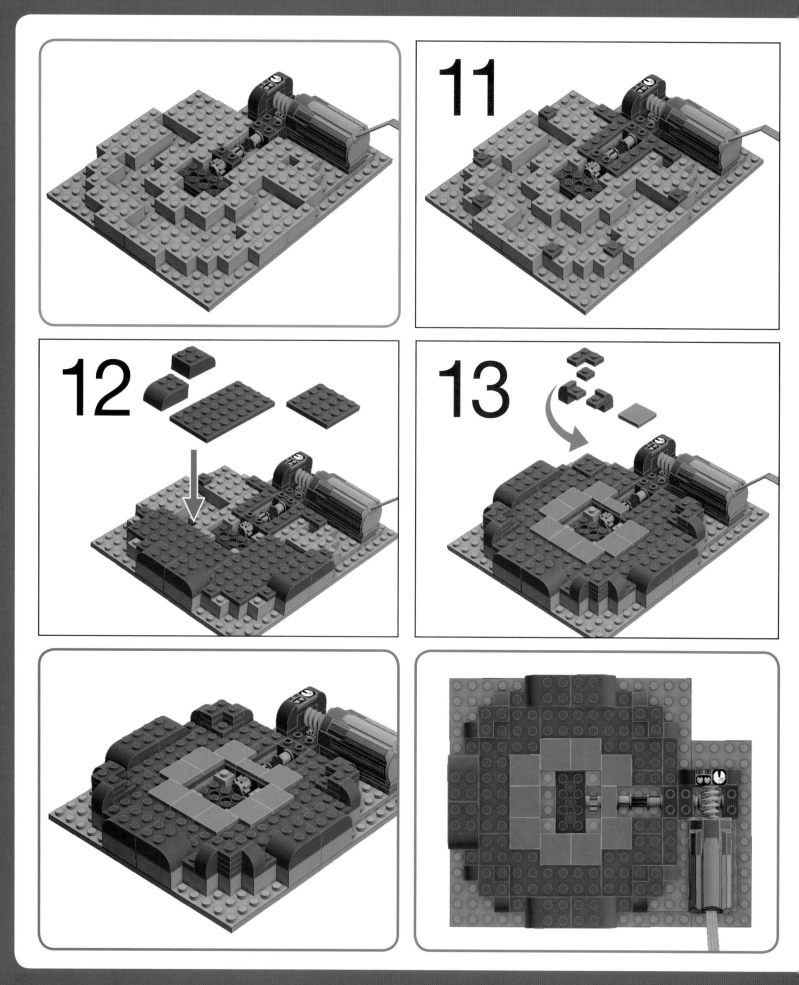

Rotor Module

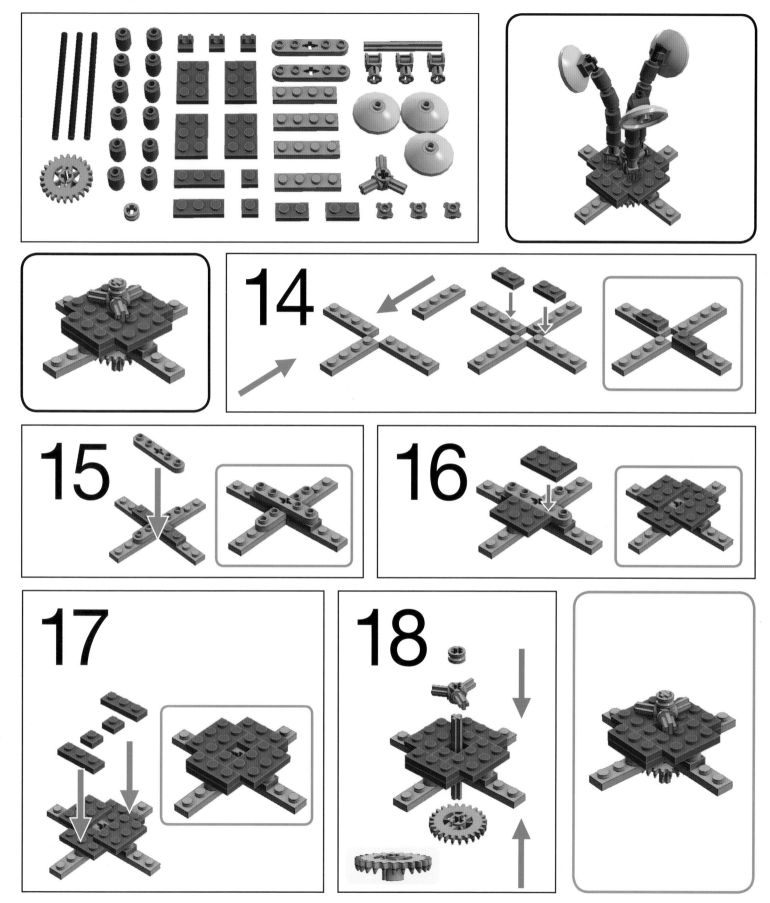

14

15

16

17

18

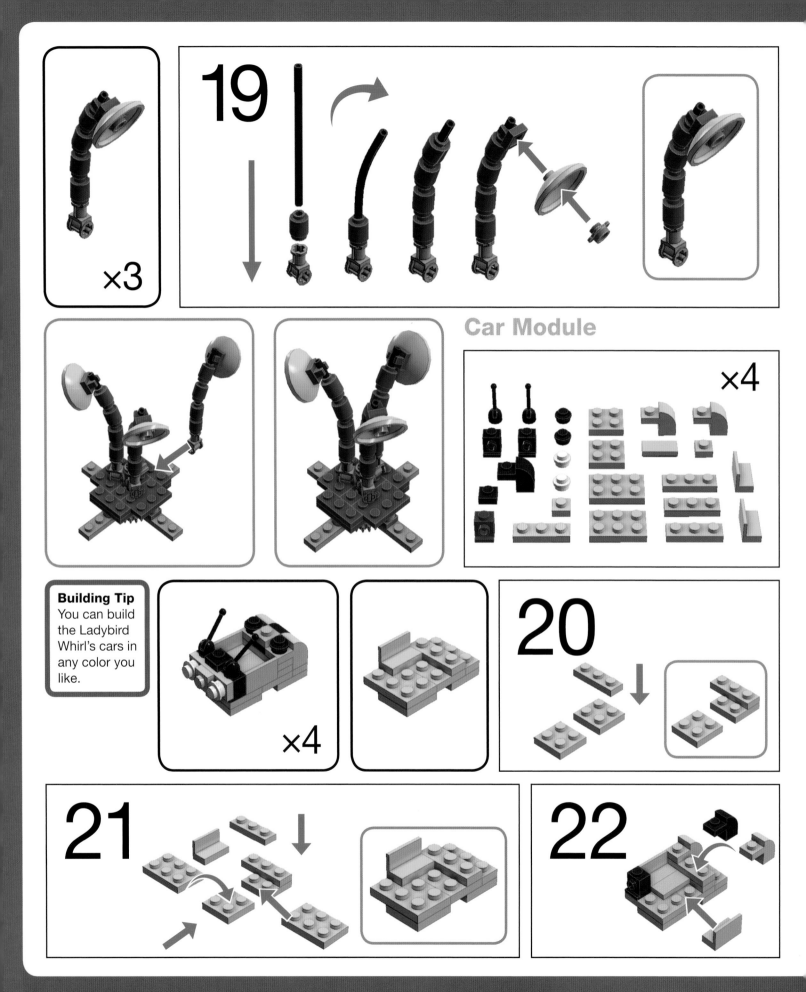

19 ×3

Car Module ×4

Building Tip
You can build the Ladybird Whirl's cars in any color you like.

×4

20

21

22

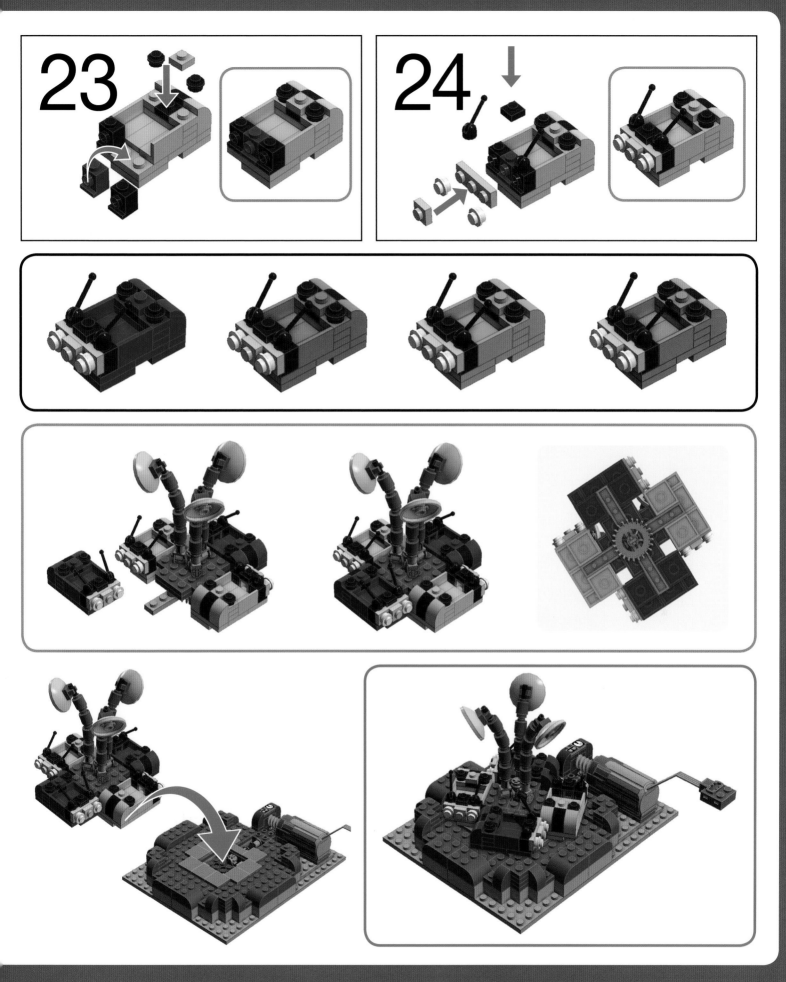

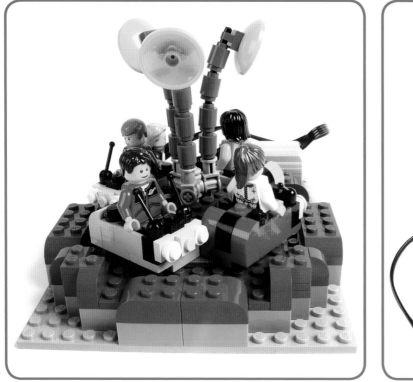

NOW THAT WE HAVE OUR RIDE OPERATOR AND COLLECTED THE TICKETS, THEY'RE READY TO GO.

WHAT A NIFTY BUILD. I'D LOVE TO SEE MORE!

NO TROUBLE THERE, MEGS. WE'VE LOTS MORE TO SEE.

Red Tractor

Traction Engine

THIS TRACTOR IS STEAM-POWERED.

OH INTERESTING, I WONDER IF THAT'S WHERE SOME OF THE INSPIRATION FOR STEAMPUNK COMES FROM?

ERHM, MAYBE, BUT THIS ISN'T STEAMPUNK, JUST REGULAR OLD STEAM!

Engine Shed

  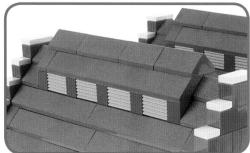

Boiler House

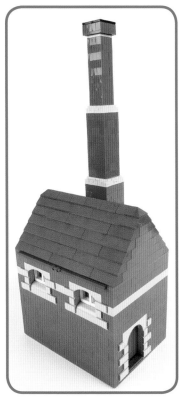 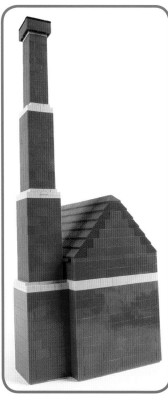 

Scots Pine Tree

Trains

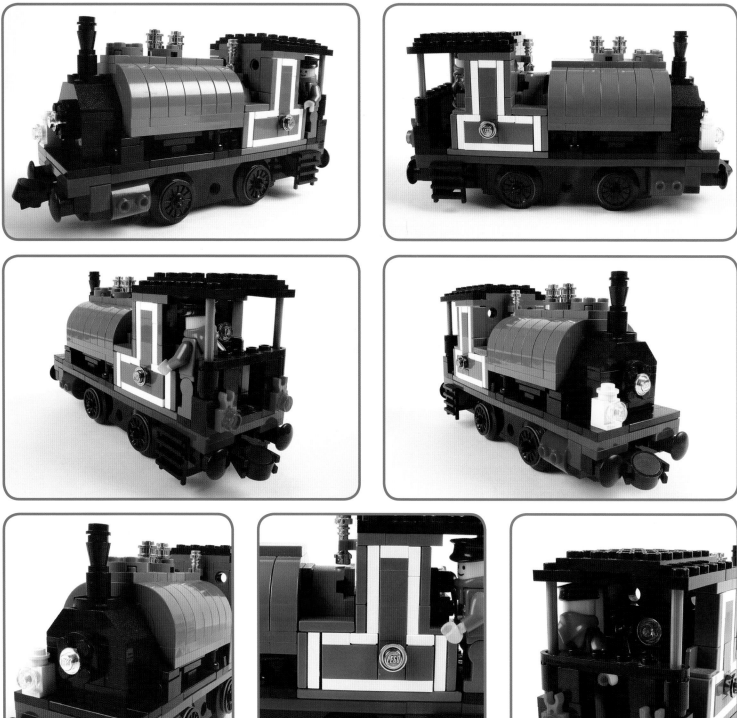

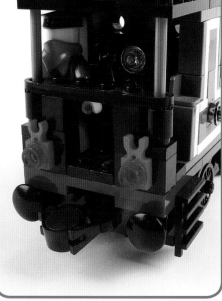

Building Tip
Instead of building a large diesel or electric locomotive, try building a smaller steam engine straight onto the motor module. Use your favorite color for the bodywork and just use black for all the little details. Remember to leave a gap for the engine's cable to come out at the back. If you're using a battery box, it can be hidden in a wagon that follows the engine.

Classic Ice Cream Van

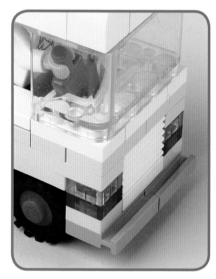

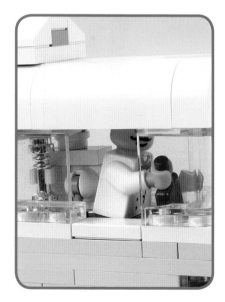

British Phone Box

Scouts

BUILDING JOURNAL

Jason's fair models are fabulous! He's put a lot of time into planning how things will move and function. Adding gears and motors really brings his models to life. Jason told me that he likes to use a lot of plates to sculpt shapes, as he did for the muscles on his Shire horses. His use of different colored ladybirds with pink noses adds a sense of whimsy, perfect for a fun fair ride!

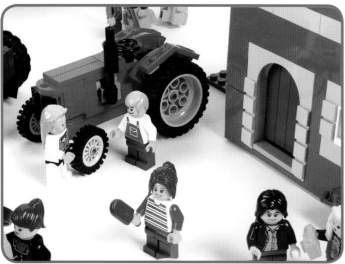

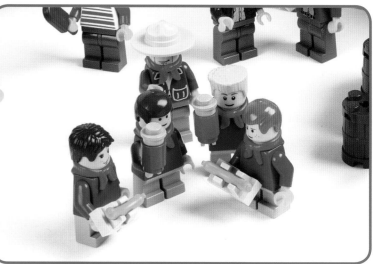

Out of Scale!

Stephan Sander

Nickname: x_Speed!

Profession: IT Specialist

Nationality: German

Website: www.x-brick.de/

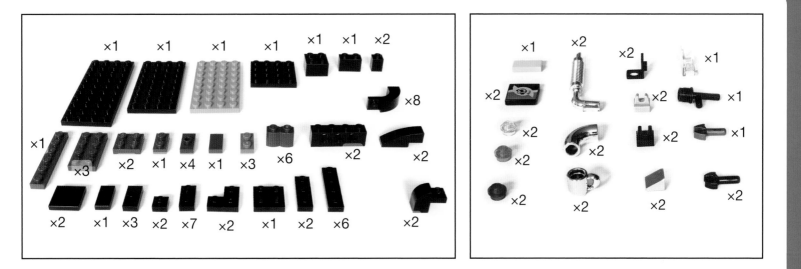

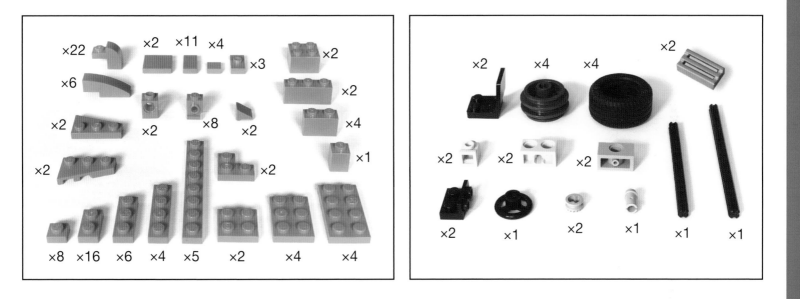

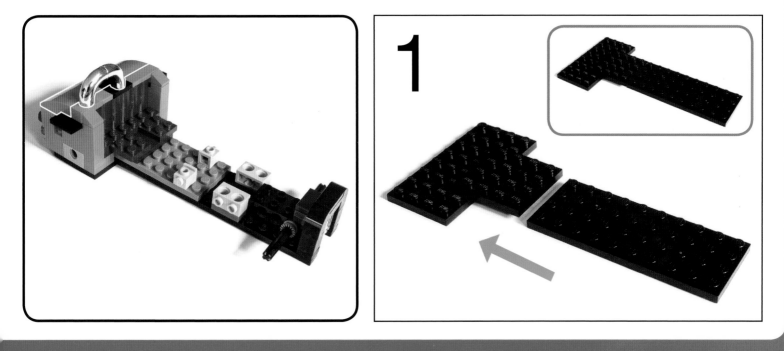

1

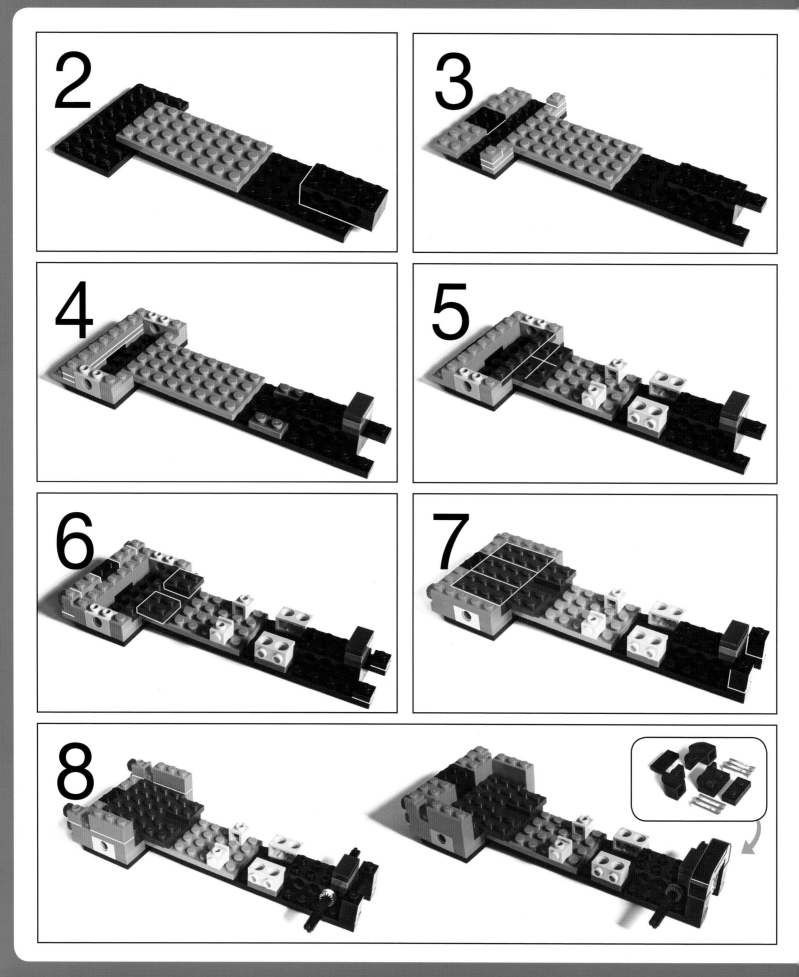

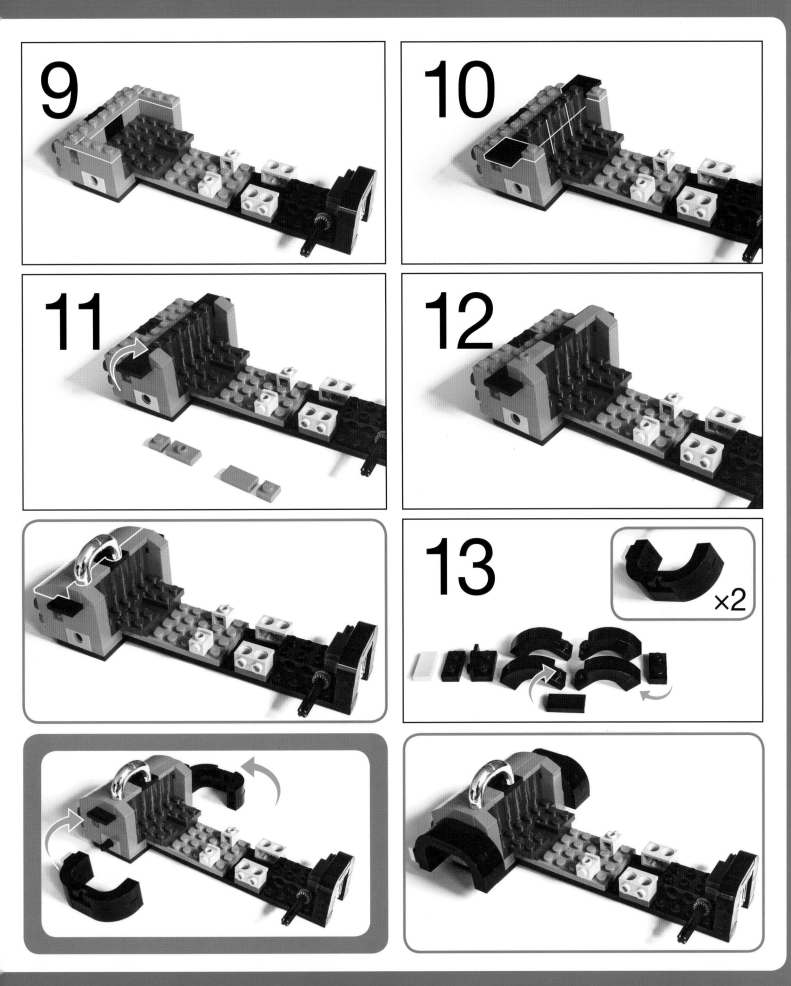

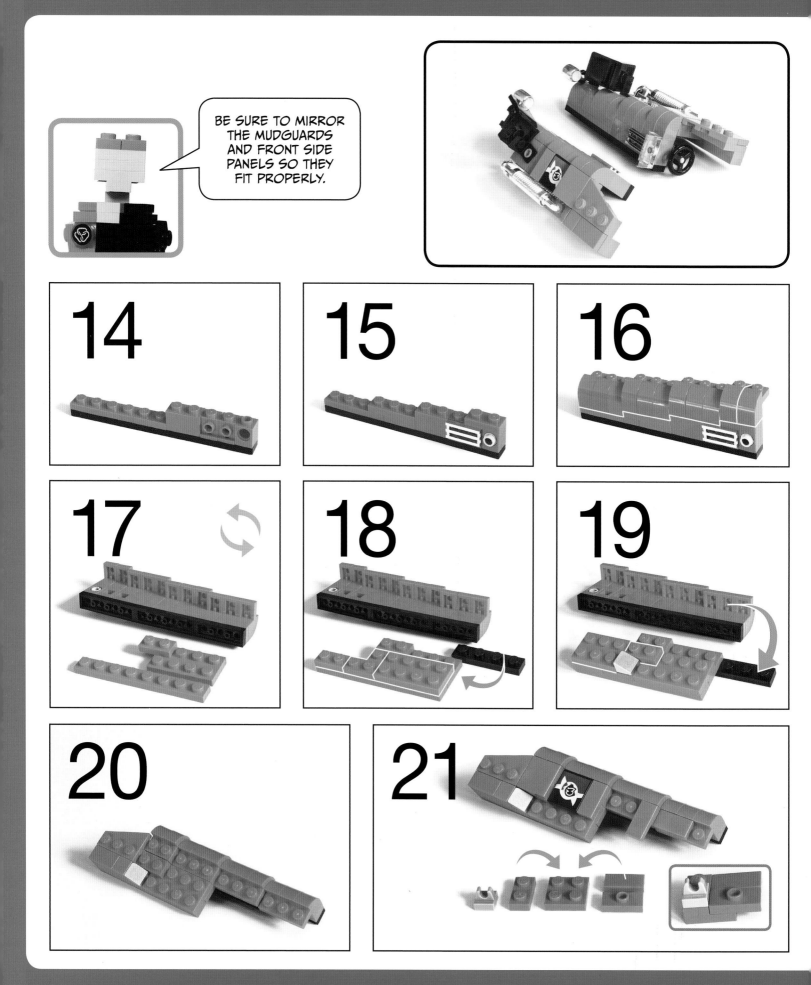

BE SURE TO MIRROR THE MUDGUARDS AND FRONT SIDE PANELS SO THEY FIT PROPERLY.

14

15

16

17

18

19

20

21

HERE'S ANOTHER VERSION OF MY LEGO SUPER 7. I BUILT THIS ONE IN DARK RACING GREEN. IT CAN BE FUN TO BUILD THE SAME TYPE OF CAR USING A DIFFERENT COLOR SCHEME.

VEHICLES COME IN ALL SHAPES, SIZES, AND COLORS. HERE ARE A FEW THAT HAVE BEEN DRIVING AROUND MY CITY'S STREETS.

Classic Rides

Fiery Stallions

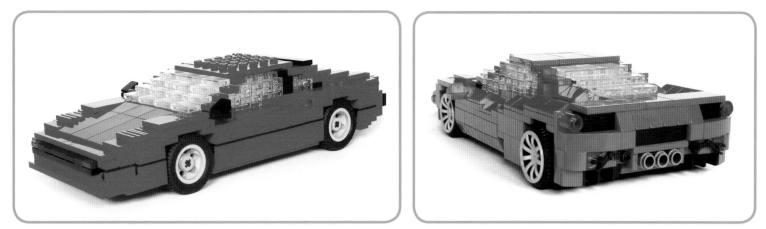

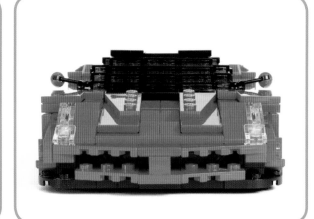

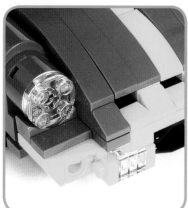

Building Tip
Capture those curves! Working with sloped elements like the ones on the right will give your ride a smooth, aerodynamic look.

Supercars

Street Rides

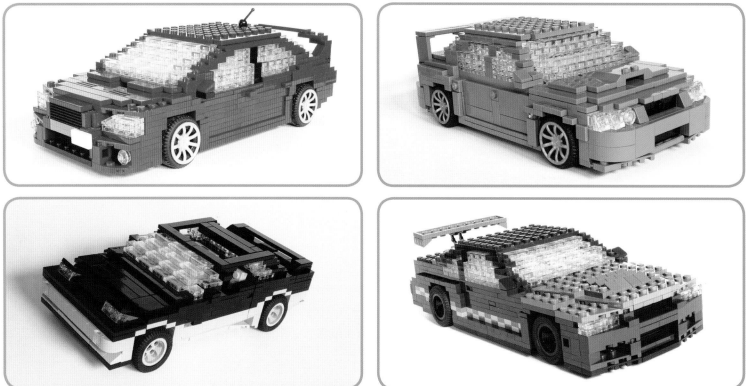

Time Machine

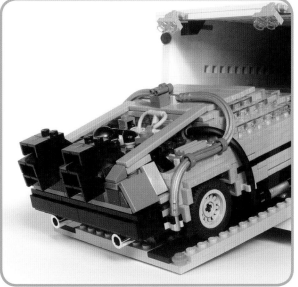

My time machine is the perfect crossover. It was inspired by a certain traveling doctor in a blue police box and another traveling doc who created a souped-up sports car in the 1980s...

Building Tip
Starting off by building a strong chassis for your vehicle. It will make a good base to build on and will keep your car nice and stable.

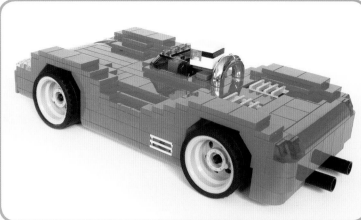

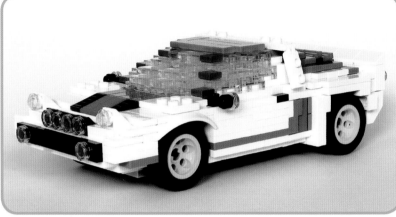

BUILDING JOURNAL

Stephan's Miniland scale vehicles are ace! He said it can take many attempts to get a car just right. Building one can require hundreds of LEGO bricks to achieve the right look and feel. Paying close attention to the shape, contour, and lines of the real versions is very important. I wonder how my Idea Truck would look in Miniland scale!

Hollywood Inspiration

Setting the Scale-o-Matic to reverse. Targeting . . . ZAPP! Grrrrr! Come back here, you Pink Nightmare!

SNAP! ZAP!

WHAT?! I'M MINIFIG SCALE AGAIN?! OH BLOKS! BETTER BOOK IT!

Brickbot to Megs, the Destructor has been demagnified, and he has already disappeared. Miniland city is safe for now.

OH NO, WE JUST MISSED HIM! WELL, NICE TRY. SEE YOU BACK AT THE IDEA LAB, BRICKBOT.

Affirmative. There is much sorting to do, as usual.

STEPHAN, IT'S BEEN REALLY GREAT TO MEET YOU AND TOUR YOUR EPIC CITY. BUT I SHOULD GET BACK TO MY REGULAR SCALE AND CATCH THAT BLASTED DESTRUCTOR!

SURE, MEGS, ONE MOMENT...

ZAP!

SNAP!

YES, BACK IN MY GEAR! TIME TO GO!

I THINK THAT SCALE FITS YOU WELL, MEGS. IT WAS MY PLEASURE TO BE YOUR GUIDE. GOOD LUCK!

THANKS FOR THE SCALE BUILDING FUN, STEPHAN! SEE YOU!

A Seaside Situation

Alex Bidolak

Nickname: Brick-A-Lak

Profession: Master Model Builder and Police Constable

Nationality: British

Website: *www.flickr.com/photos/bidolak/sets/72157630913115524/*

WHAT ON EARTH HAPPENED, TAD DARLING?

A FREAK WAVE MAYBE?

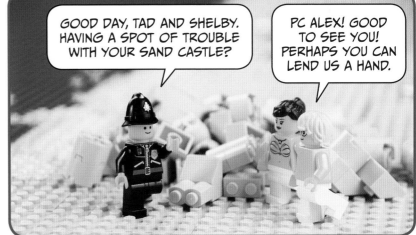

GOOD DAY, TAD AND SHELBY. HAVING A SPOT OF TROUBLE WITH YOUR SAND CASTLE?

PC ALEX! GOOD TO SEE YOU! PERHAPS YOU CAN LEND US A HAND.

WE TURNED OUR BACKS FOR A MOMENT, AND OUR SAND CASTLE WAS DESTROYED! WE BELIEVE A FREAK WAVE TO BE THE CULPRIT.

HELLO THERE, I'M MEGS. I'M AFRAID IT WAS ACTUALLY THE WORK OF THE DESTRUCTOR, A RATHER MEAN-TEMPERED CHAP WHO LIKES TO DESTROY NICE THINGS!

HELLO, MEGS. PC ALEX AT YOUR SERVICE! LET'S SEE ABOUT APPREHENDING THIS PINK BADDY THEN. I SHALL CALL FOR BRICK...ER, BACKUP!

OKAY, GREAT!

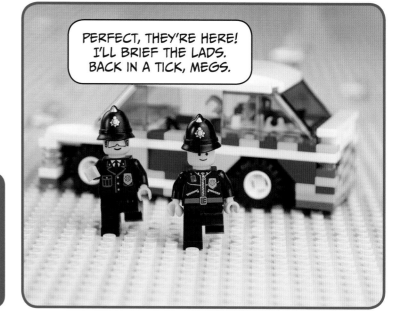

PERFECT, THEY'RE HERE! I'LL BRIEF THE LADS. BACK IN A TICK, MEGS.

RIGHT, CHAPS, CODE 221. BE ON THE LOOKOUT FOR A KNOWN BADDY: THE DESTRUCTOR. HE MAY ALSO HAVE HIS CREW, THE BAD-BOTS, IN TOW. HE IS A SLIPPERY BLOKE, SO USE CAUTION WHEN APPREHENDING HIM.

AH, SIR, WHAT ARE HIS CRIMES?

DESTROYING LOVELY LEGO MODELS FROM ALL OVER, LIKE THAT NICE SAND CASTLE OF TAD AND SHELBY'S. I WILL HELP MEGS SORT OUT THIS MESS. LEAVE NO BRICK UNTURNED!

Sand Castle

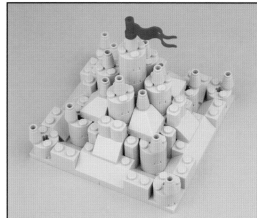

NO WORRIES ABOUT BUILDING THIS SAND CASTLE. JUST BE SURE TO START WITH THE BASE AND STACK AWAY. YOU WON'T EVEN GET YOUR FINGERS GRITTY WITH THIS BUILD.

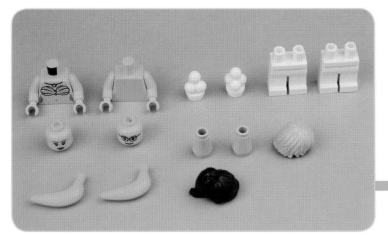

Building Tip

When building a solid object like a sand castle, start by working out a base to stack on, just as you would when building a real sand castle.

1

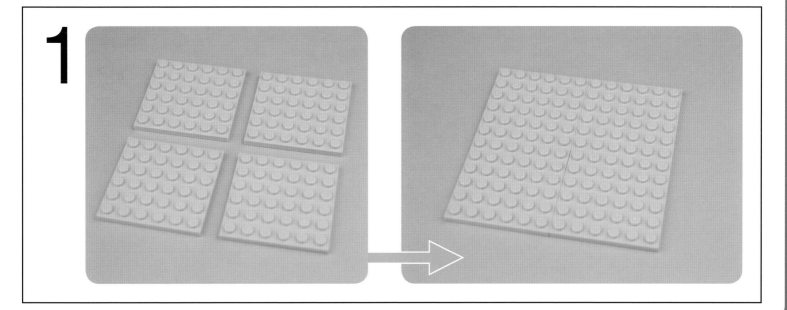

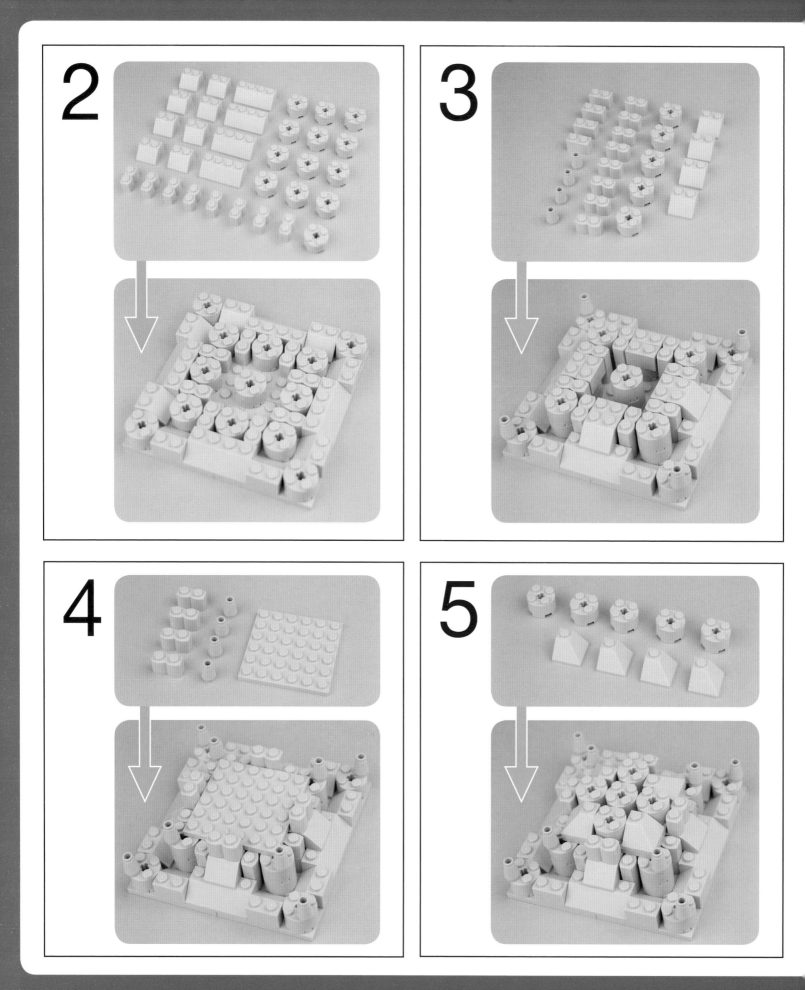

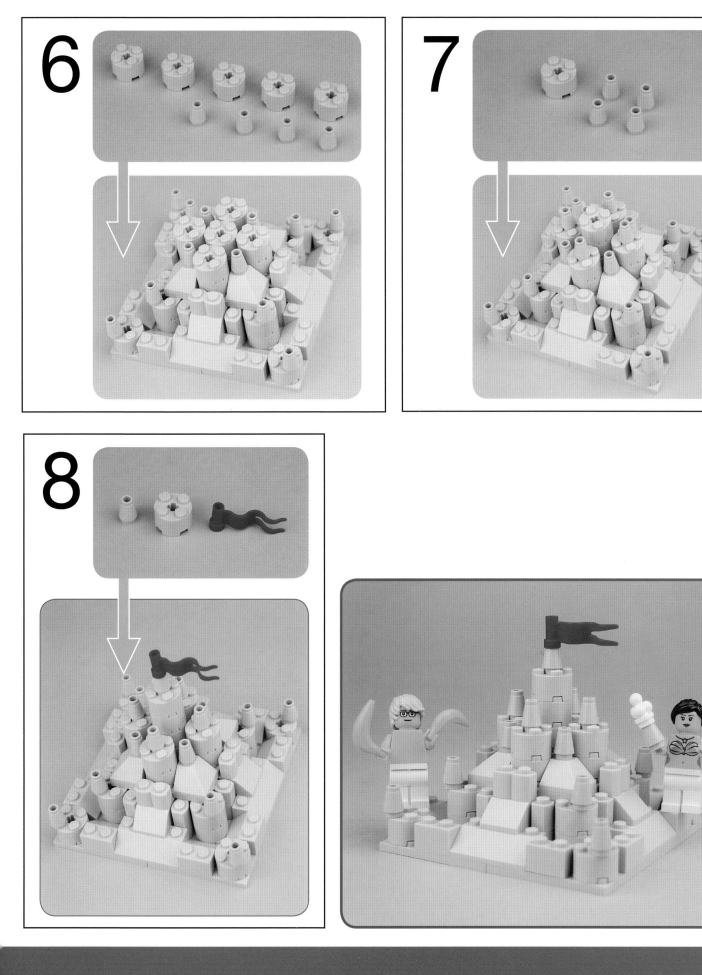

Ice Cream Van

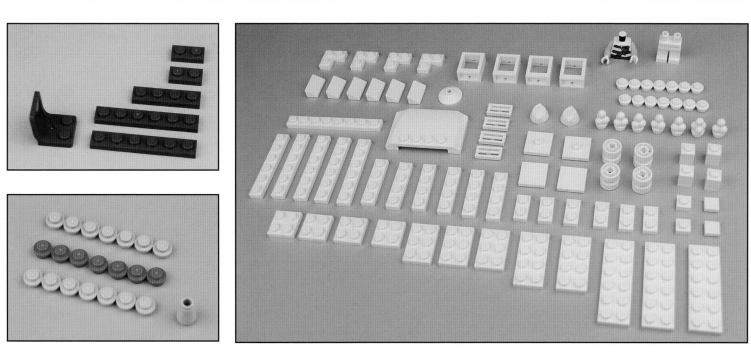

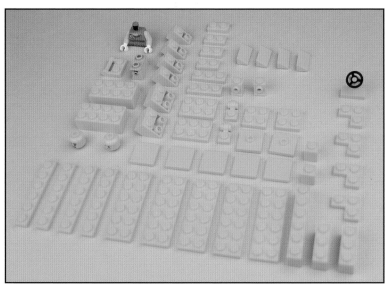

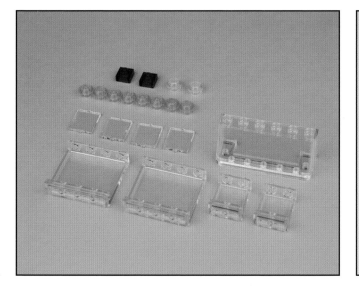

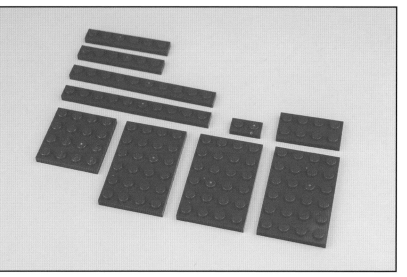

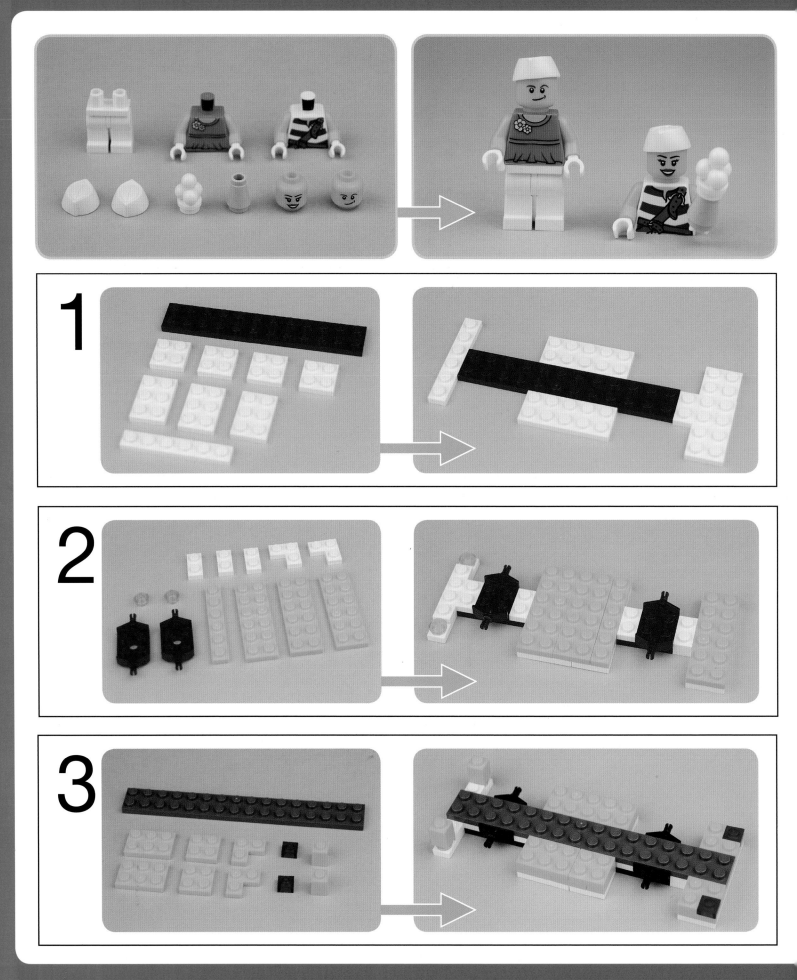

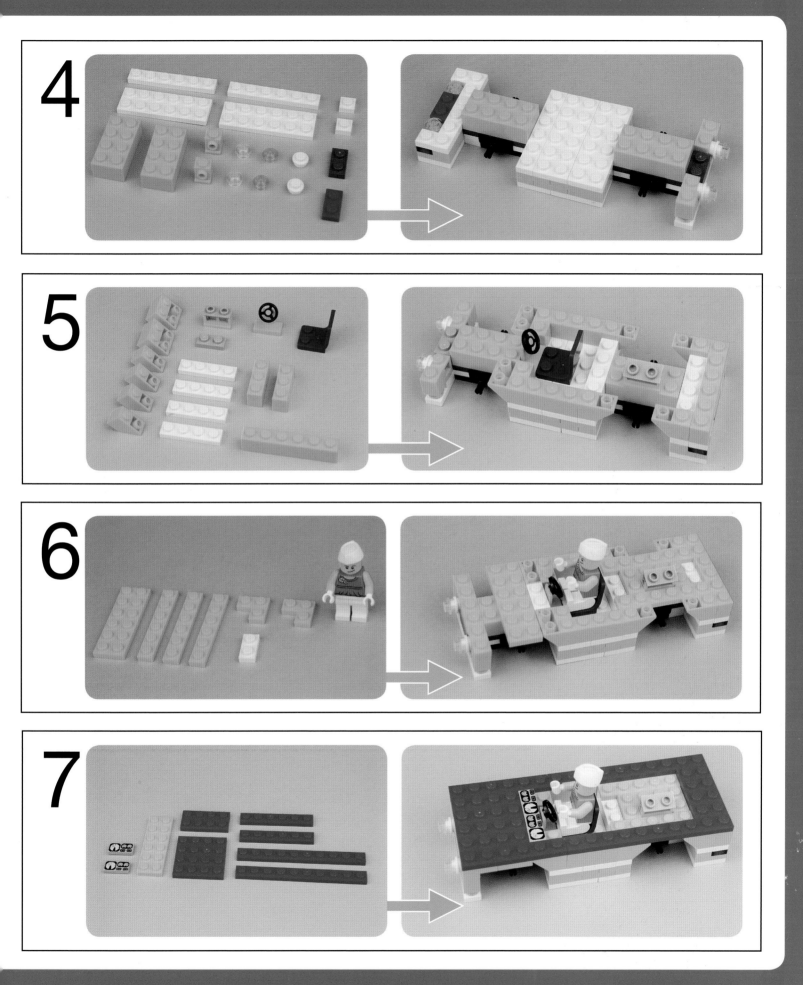

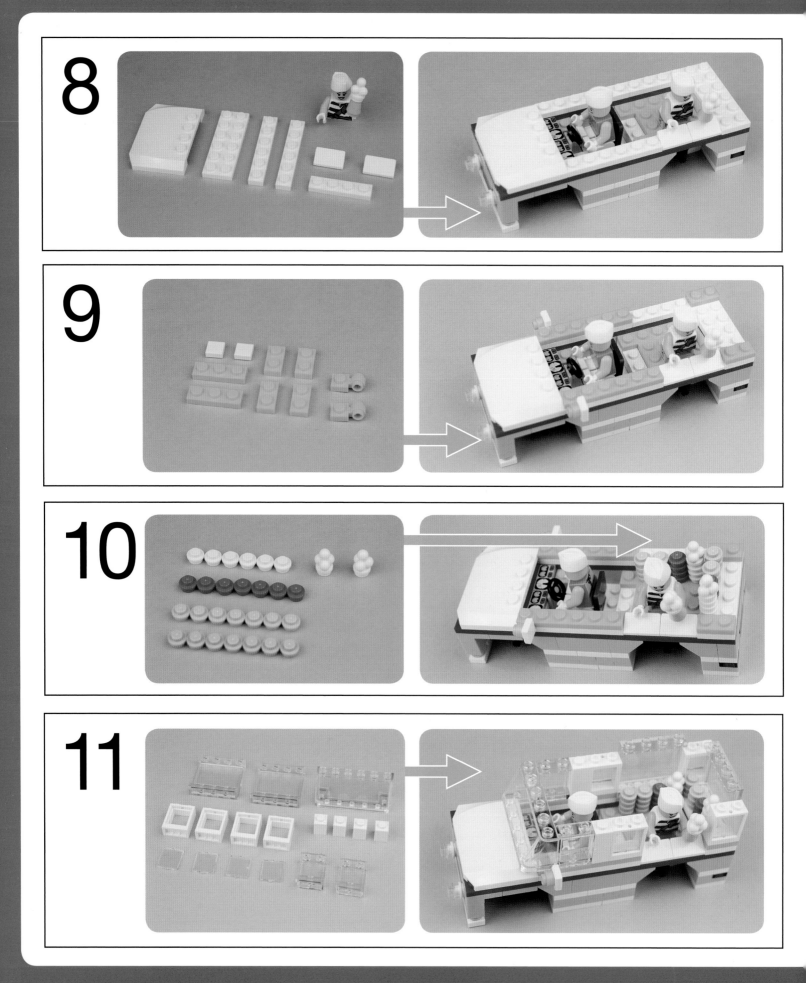

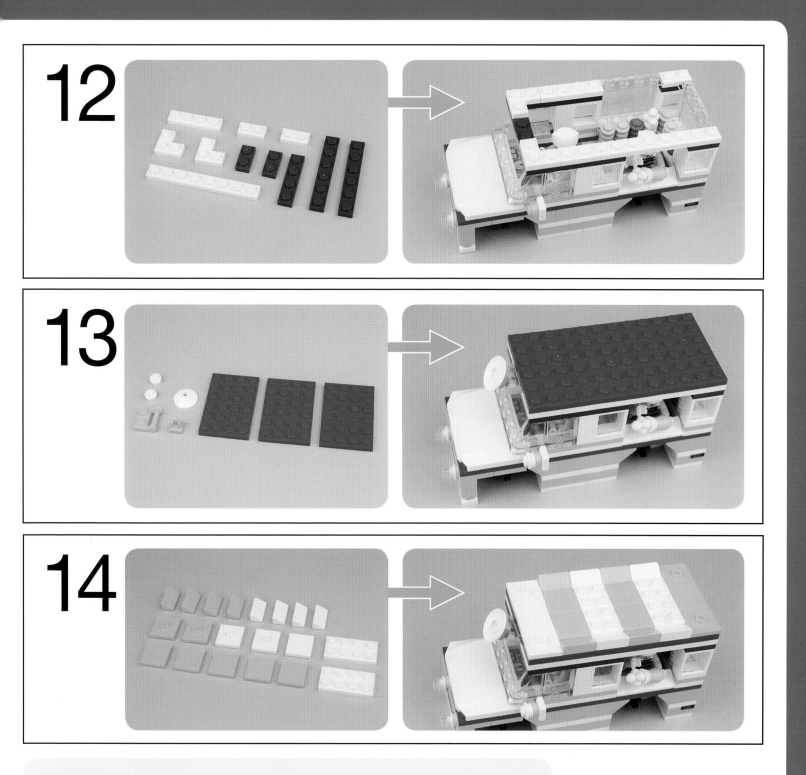

BUILDING JOURNAL

Alex draws a lot of inspiration from his daily life. Living in Manchester in the United Kingdom, he explores the city and builds local landmarks and vehicles out of LEGO bricks. "What I love most about building is that there are loads of building solutions to choose from. LEGO bricks are a universal form of playing and learning. For me, LEGO building is more than just playtime; it is a timeless, versatile, and creative art form."

Building Tip
With a few color changes, you can transform the look and feel of your truck. For example, adding colors like greens and purples gives you a flower delivery truck, while adding some red, orange, and more yellow can transform it into a food truck.

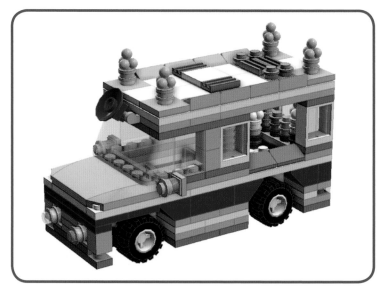

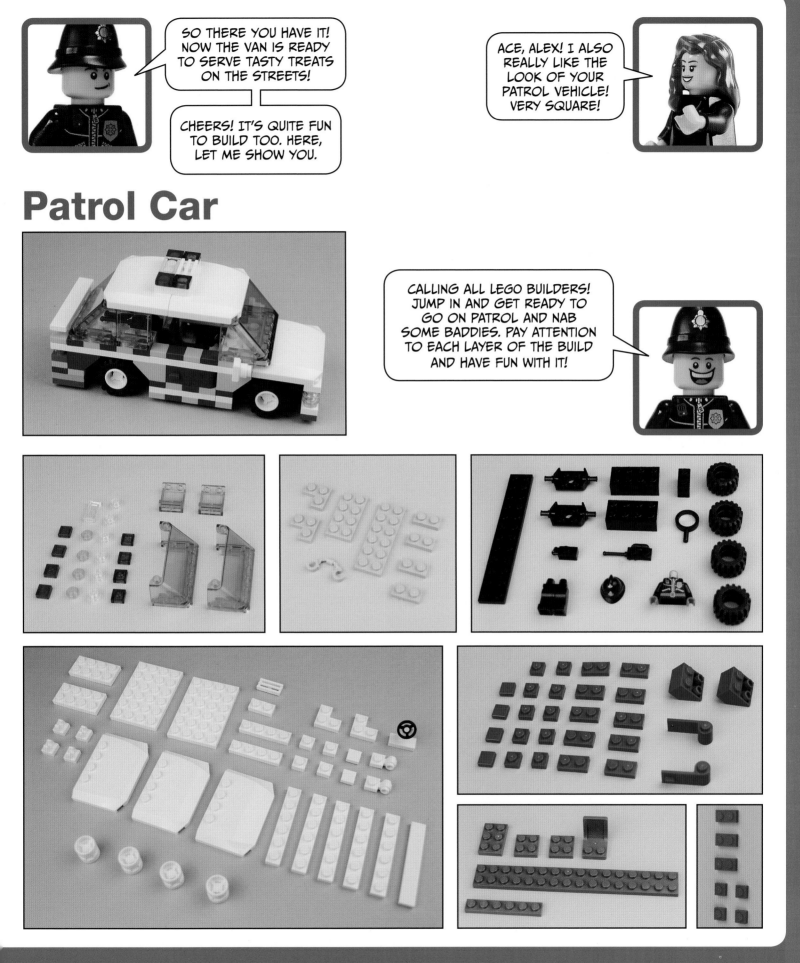

Patrol Car

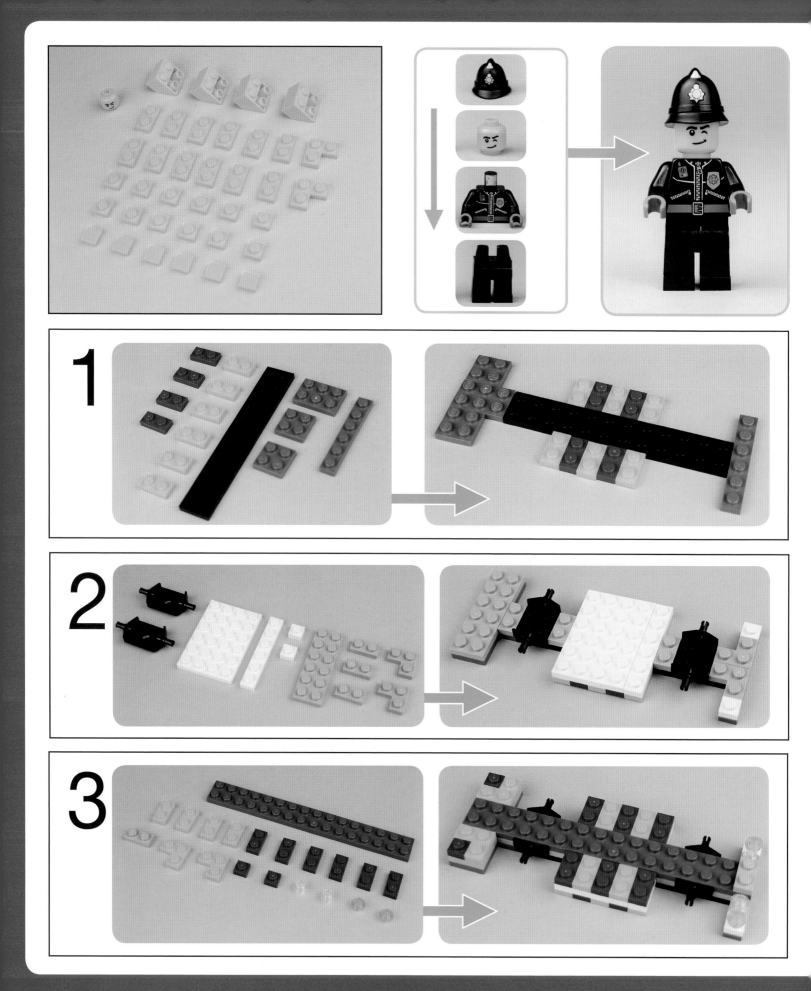

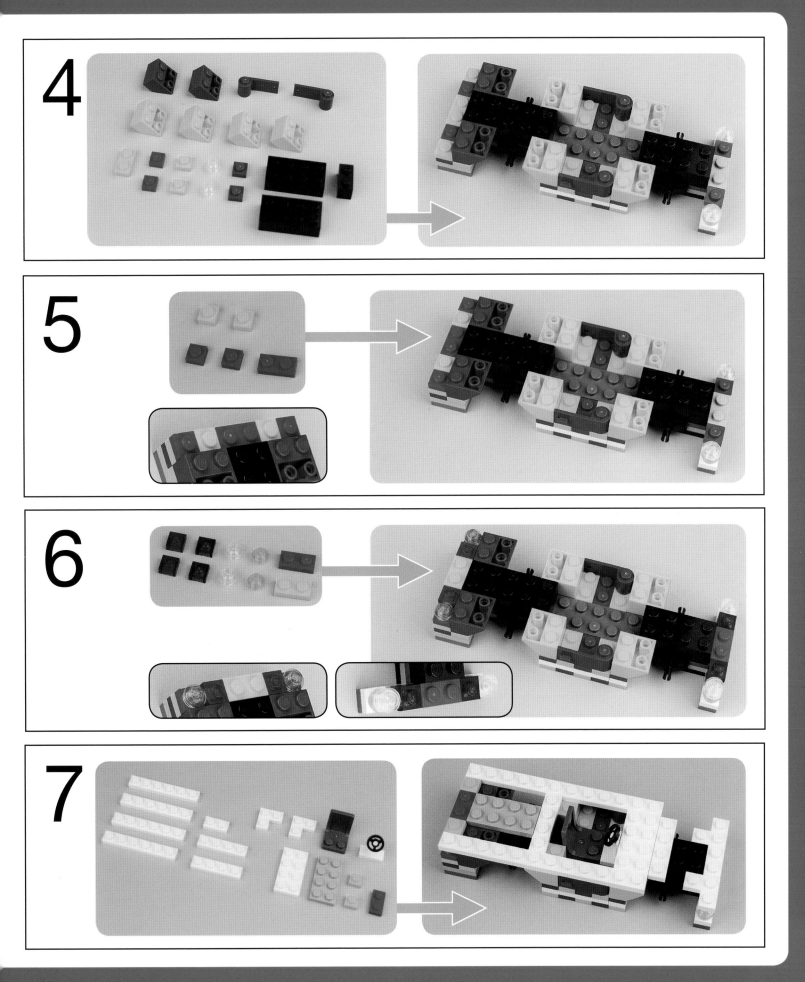

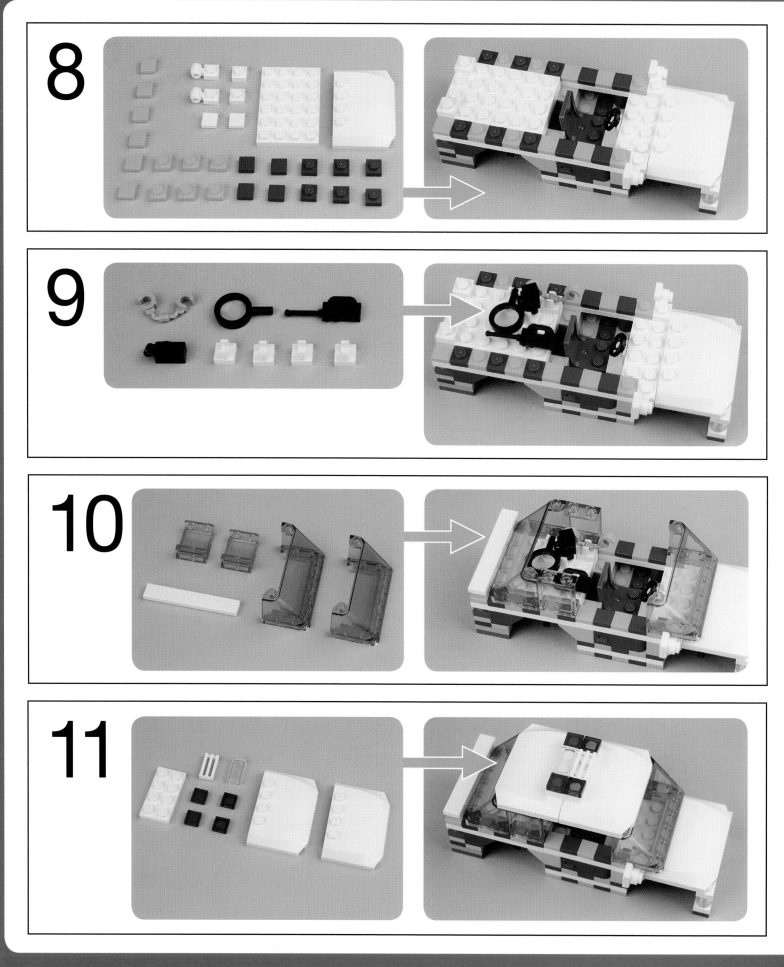

12

Building Tip

Using inverted 1×2 slopes and stepping out by two studs from the inside of the chassis is a simple and clean way to build in a fender.

IN NEED OF A CIVILIAN VEHICLE? TRY SWAPPING OUT SOME YELLOW AND ADDING BLACK AND WHITE BITS, AND YOU'LL HAVE A TAXI!

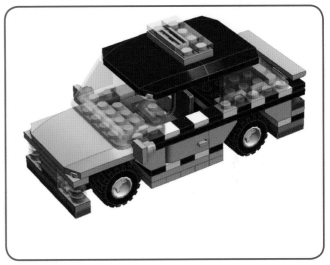

Taxi Stand

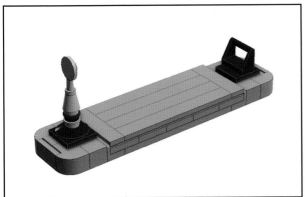

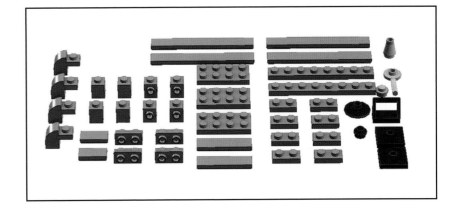

BUILDING JOURNAL

Alex's LEGO models are ace! He told me, "I like to build from my imagination. I often reflect upon my own childhood, thinking about those amazing LEGO models I could only dream about building then." He starts most of his LEGO models by sketching on specially designed LEGO brick paper and later works with real LEGO bricks.

He says always keeping a sketchbook nearby is a great way to record all of your ideas, and having your LEGO bricks sorted will speed up your building productivity. "Don't be afraid to share your ideas with your friends and family. Have fun and never stop building!" Like me, his hope is to inspire future LEGO model builders, and I think he is well on his way there!

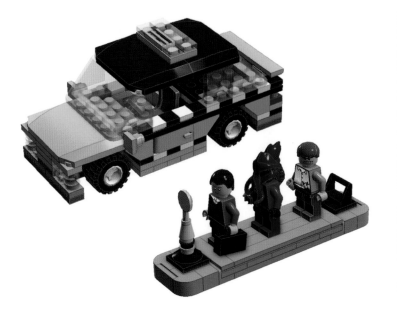

Building Tip
Using two colors of 1×2 plates results in a nice checkerboard pattern for the side of your vehicle. You can add a pretty slick pinstripe in a single contrasting color.

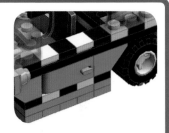

WELL, ALEX, SOME REALLY NICE WORK THERE! ISN'T IT AWESOME HOW A FEW COLOR CHANGES HAVE TURNED YOUR PATROL CAR INTO A TAXI? THAT'S LEGO MAGIC FOR YOU!

SOUNDS GOOD! LEAD ON.

YES, INDEED, MEGS! LEGO BRICKS ARE SO INSPIRING TO ME. I JUST LOVE 'EM! NOW I'VE A SPECIAL SURPRISE— A RATHER WELL-KNOWN SPOT IN THESE PARTS. LET'S POP AROUND THE CORNER AND 'AVE A LOOK!

THE WOOLPACK INN IS A LOCAL TREASURE, LOCATED JUST OUTSIDE OF TOWN. FOLKS HERE HAVE BEEN KNOWN TO KICK UP QUITE A BIT OF DUST.

Building Tip
Using different colored bricks and plates in a similar color scheme and stepping out half a stud with tiles will create a nice old-wall effect for an older building.

COME IN, PC ALEX!

WE HAD THE DESTRUCTOR CORNERED, BUT THEN HE BUILT A LADDER AND SKEDADDLED!

PC ALEX HERE. GO AHEAD!

NO WORRIES, PC PLOD, YOU DID YOUR BEST. MEGS SAID HE WAS ONE SLIPPERY FISH. WE'LL MEET YOU BACK AT ORIGINAL CRIME SCENE.

159

Dinner and a Show

Matija Pužar

Nickname: Matija/Puma

Profession: LEGO Certified Professional and IT Developer

Nationality: Norwegian

Website: *www.matija.no/*

Scrumptious Sushi

YOU DON'T NEED TO BE A MASTER CHEF TO BUILD MATIJA'S MINUTE MEALS, BUT YOU DO NEED TO PAY ATTENTION TO THE STEPS.

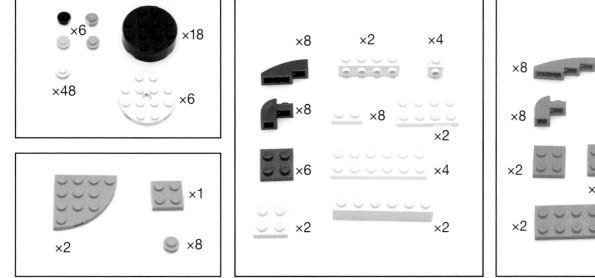

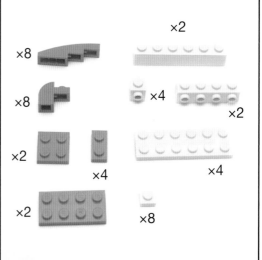

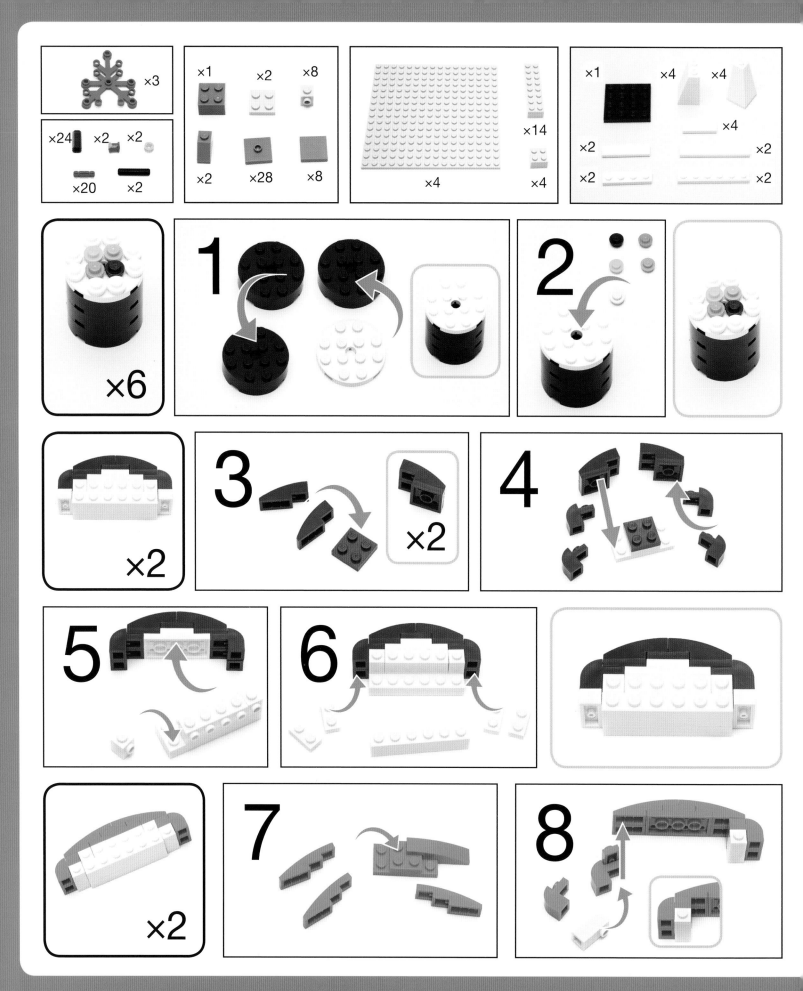

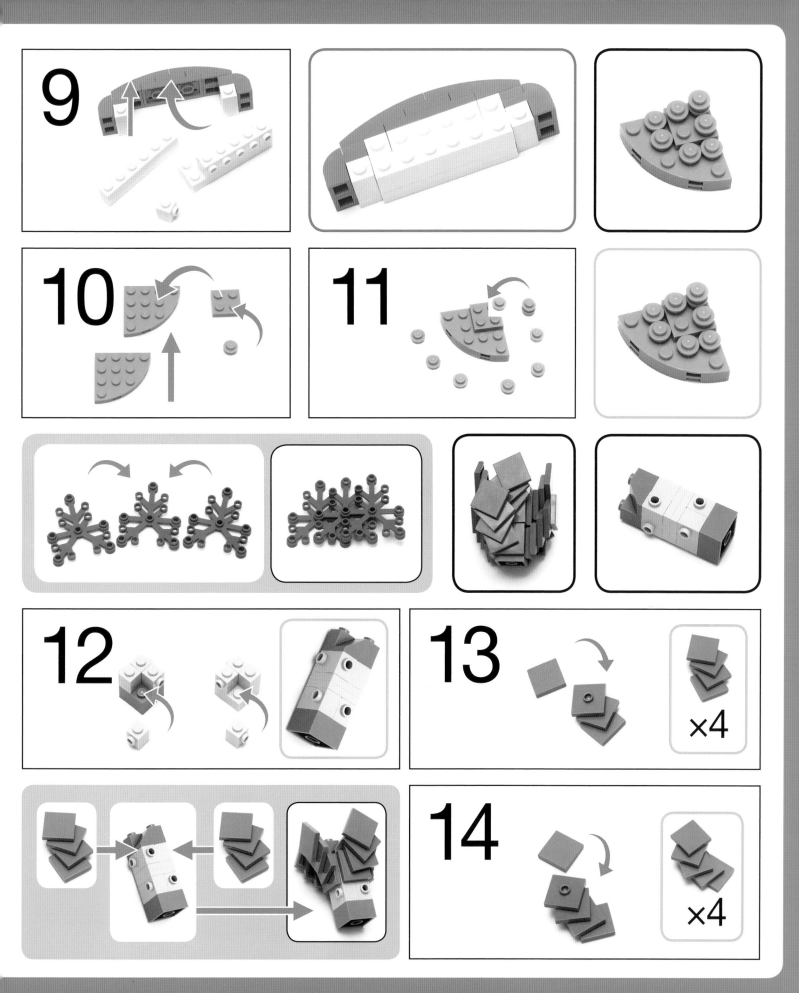

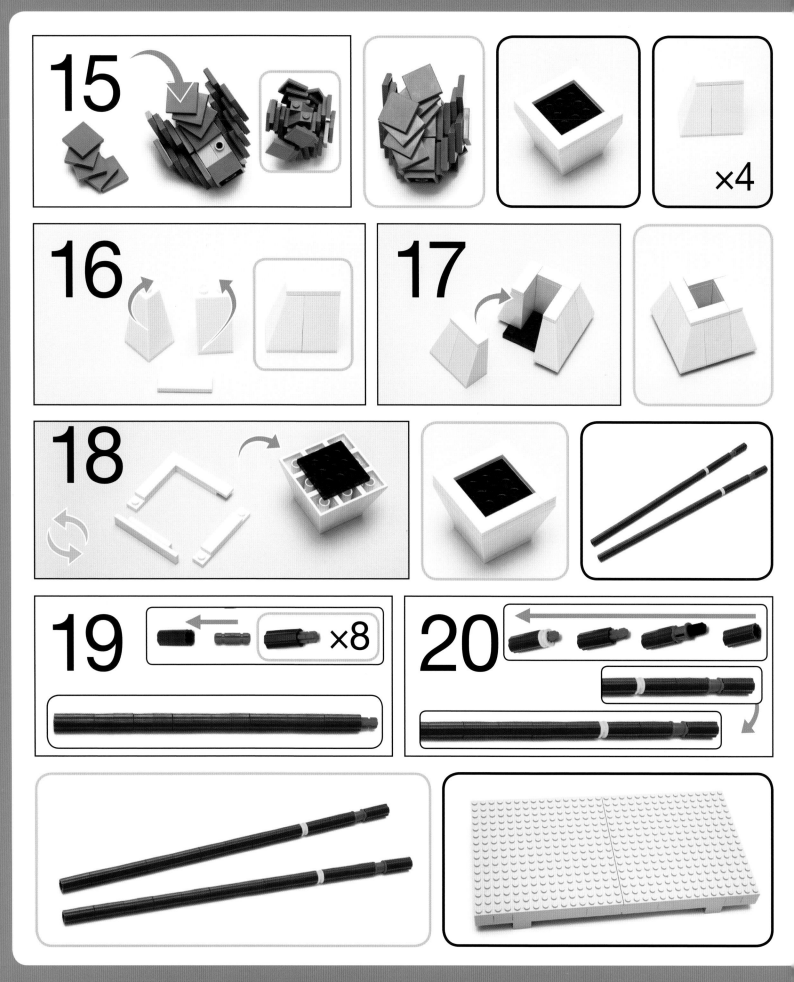

Brick Burger

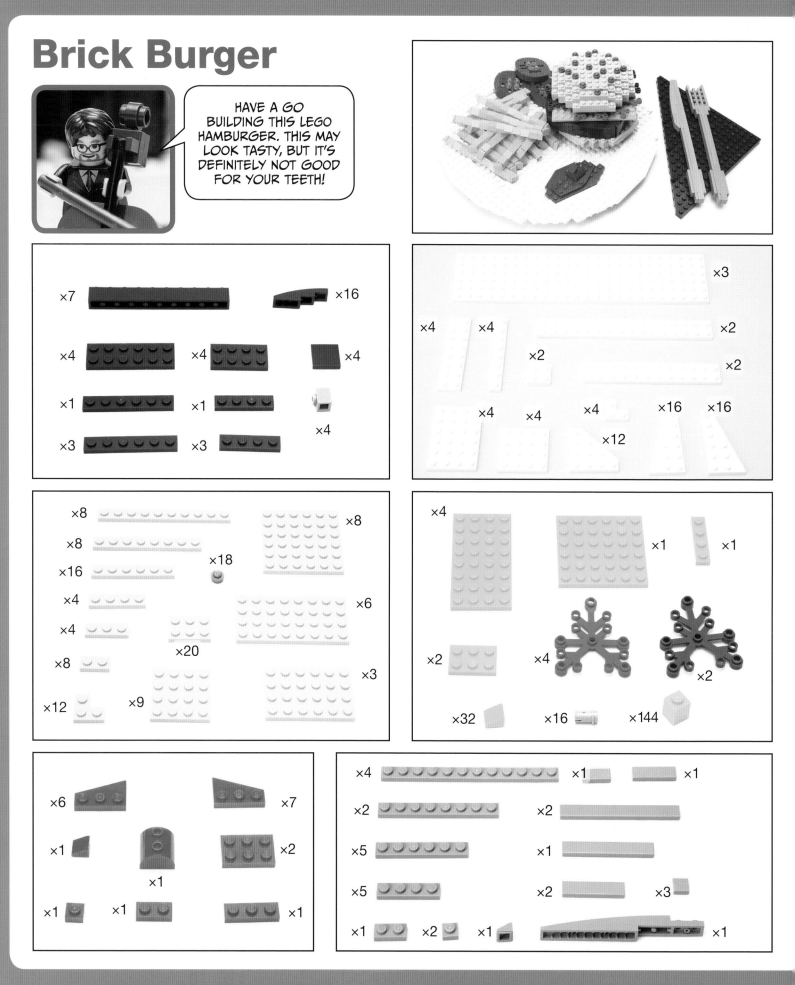

HAVE A GO BUILDING THIS LEGO HAMBURGER. THIS MAY LOOK TASTY, BUT IT'S DEFINITELY NOT GOOD FOR YOUR TEETH!

×7 ×16

×4 ×4 ×4

×1 ×1 ×4

×3 ×3

×3

×4 ×4 ×2

×2 ×2

×4 ×4 ×4 ×16 ×16

×12

×8 ×8

×8

×16 ×18

×4 ×6

×4

×20

×8

×12 ×9 ×3

×4 ×1 ×1

×2 ×4 ×2

×32 ×16 ×144

×6 ×7

×1 ×2

×1

×1 ×1 ×1

×4 ×1 ×1

×2 ×2

×5 ×1

×5 ×2 ×3

×1 ×2 ×1 ×1

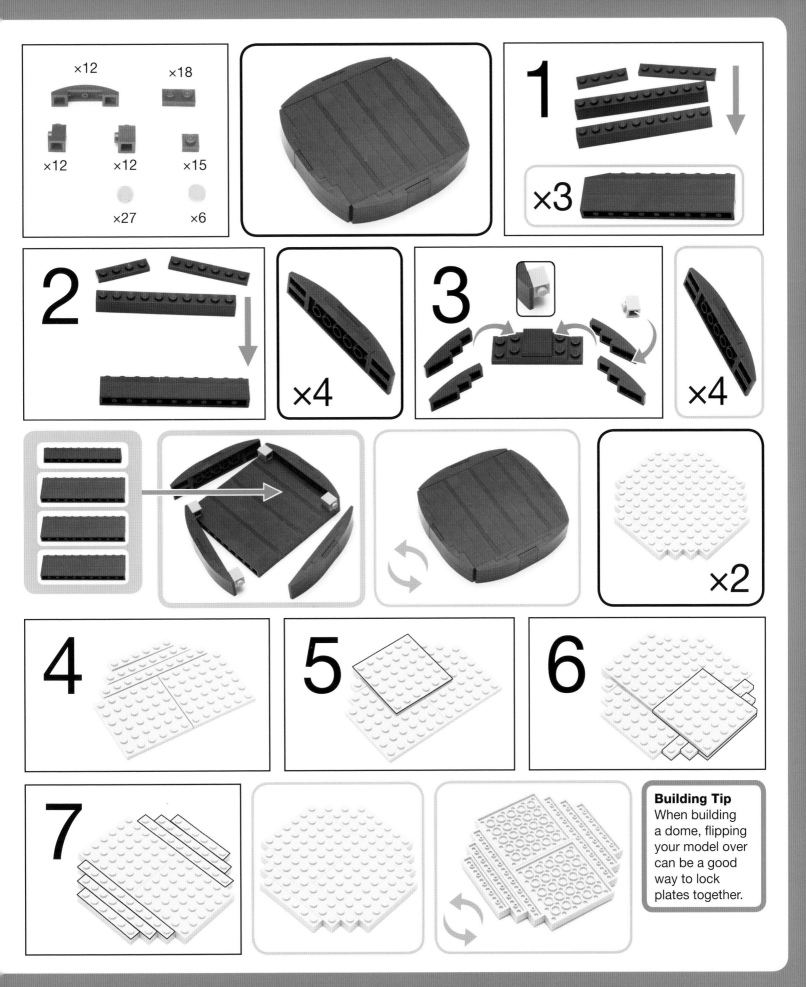

Building Tip
When building a dome, flipping your model over can be a good way to lock plates together.

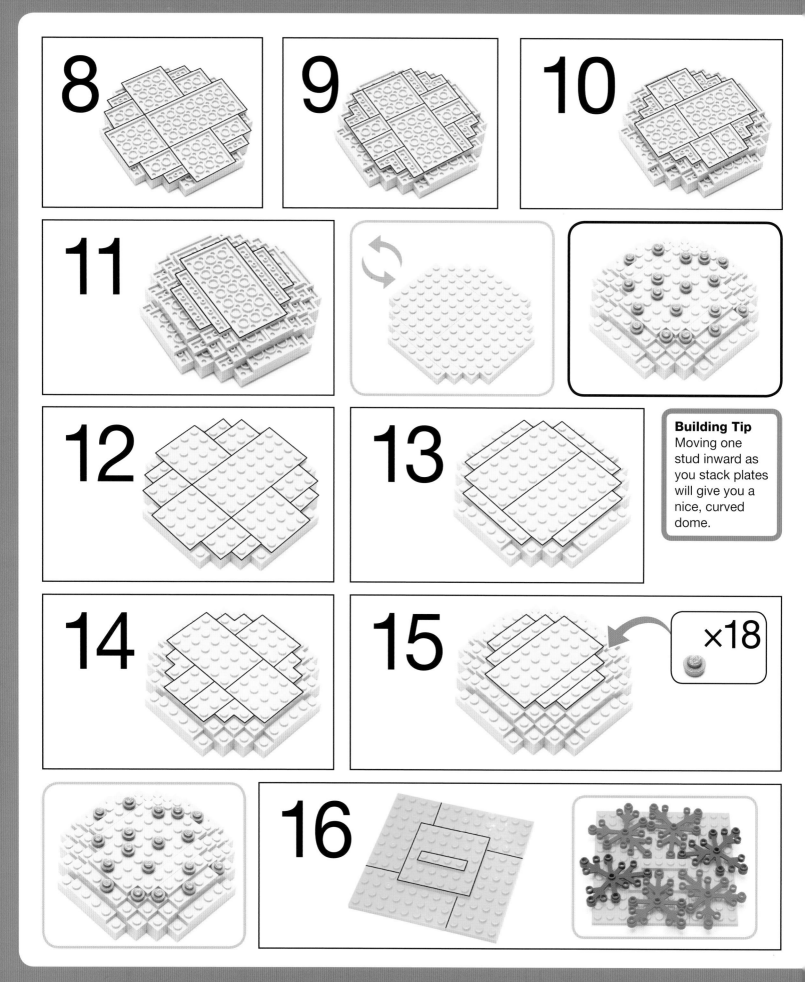

Building Tip
Moving one stud inward as you stack plates will give you a nice, curved dome.

×18

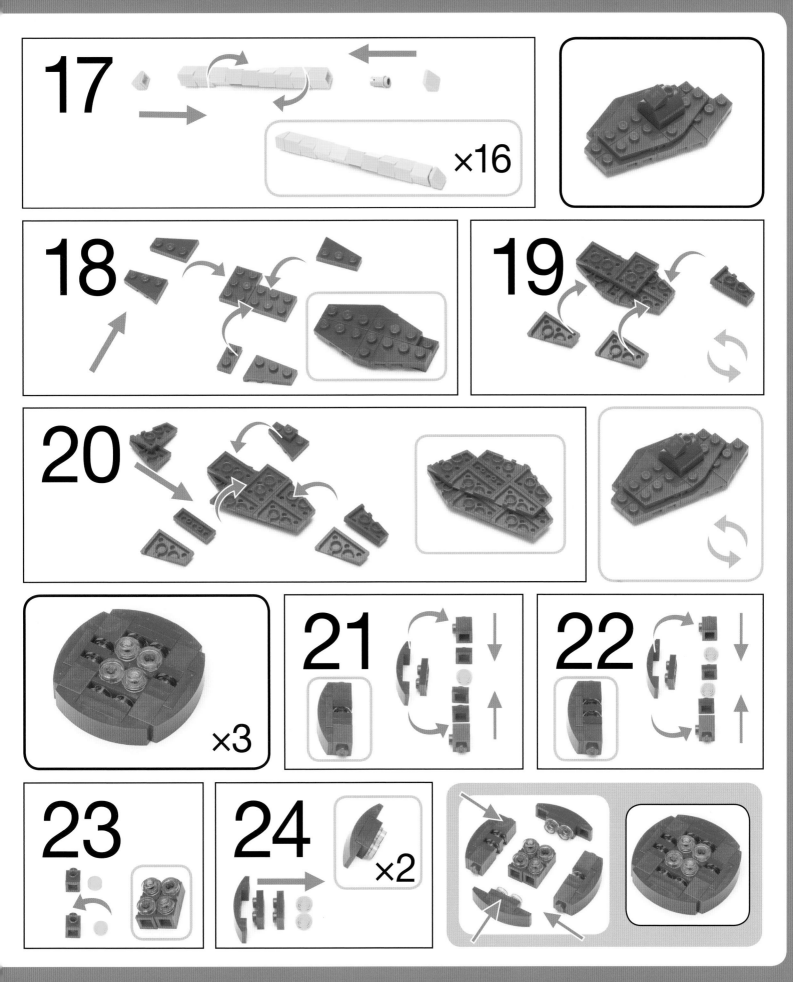

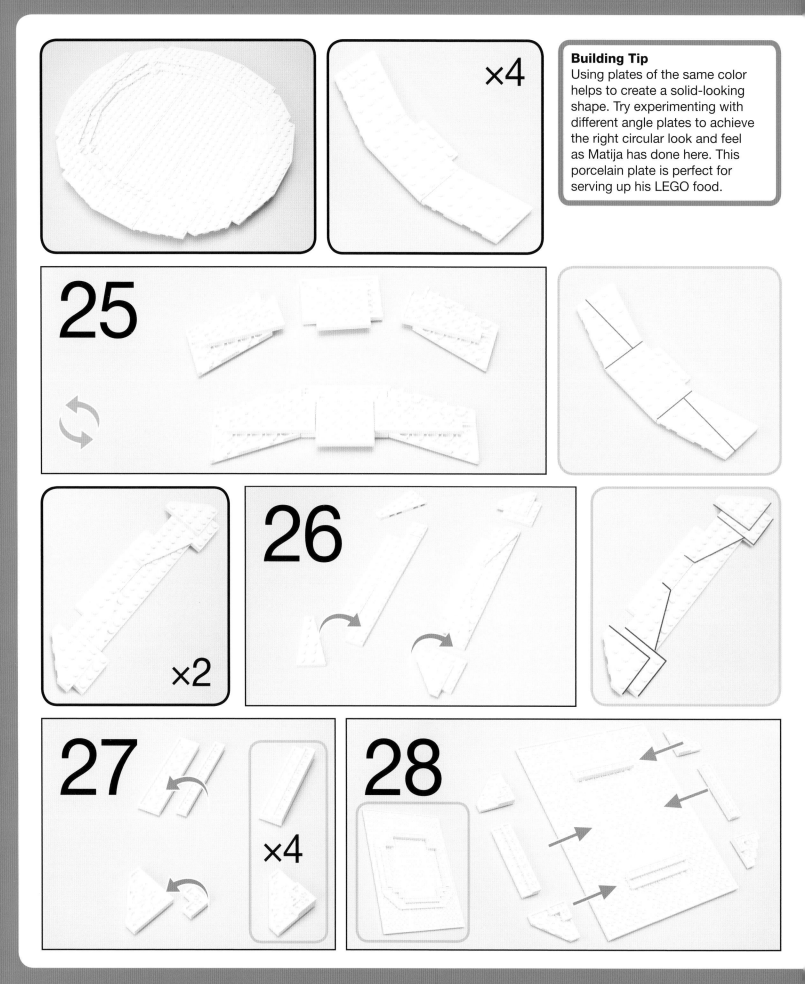

Building Tip
Using plates of the same color helps to create a solid-looking shape. Try experimenting with different angle plates to achieve the right circular look and feel as Matija has done here. This porcelain plate is perfect for serving up his LEGO food.

×4

25

26

×2

27

×4

28

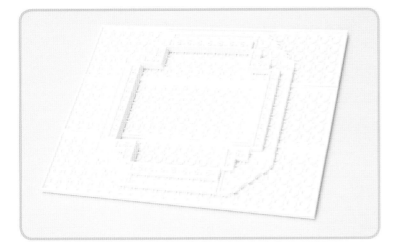

BUILDING JOURNAL

Matija's minute meals are ace! His use of 1:1 scale and choice of color schemes make his food very realistic. Combining brown with dark red on the brick burger tricks your eye into thinking it is real and fresh off the grill.

The presentation of the food on a plate just adds to the realism. Matija told me he pays close attention to the natural color, shape, and texture of food to capture it properly. Working from either reference images or real food will help you build something realistic and appetizing. I wonder if my yard could use a giant watermelon?

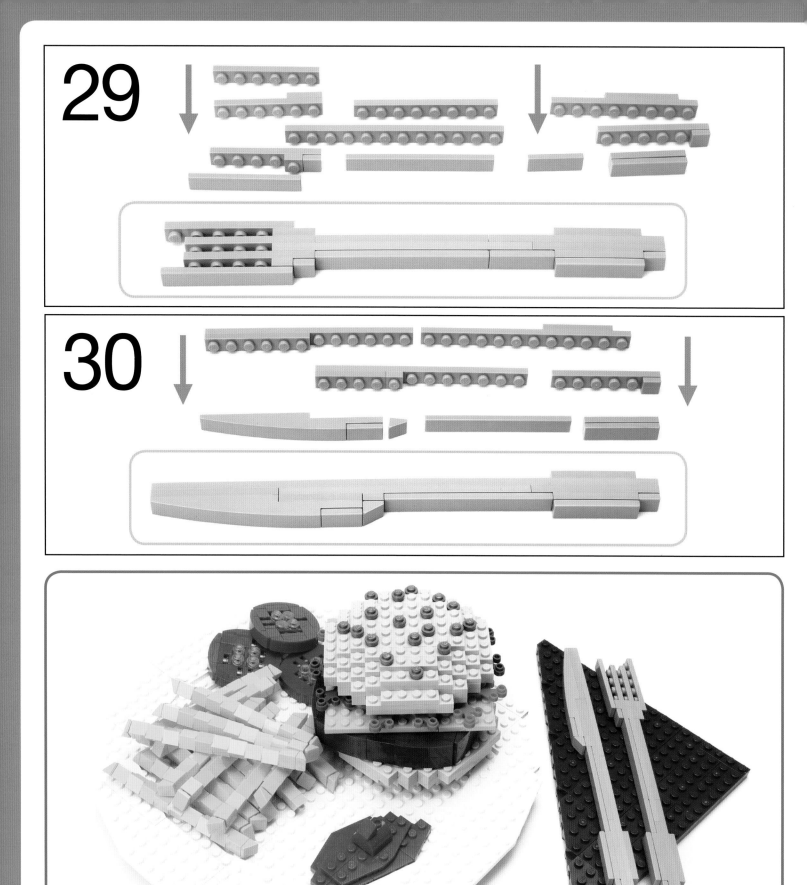

Matija's Minute Meals

At the Symphony

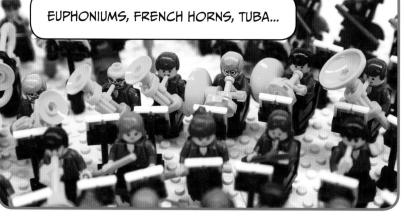

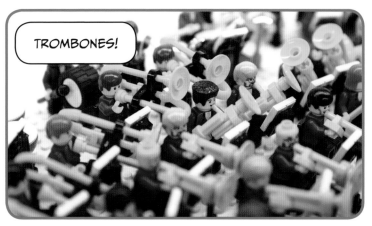

Tuba

French Horn

Double Bass

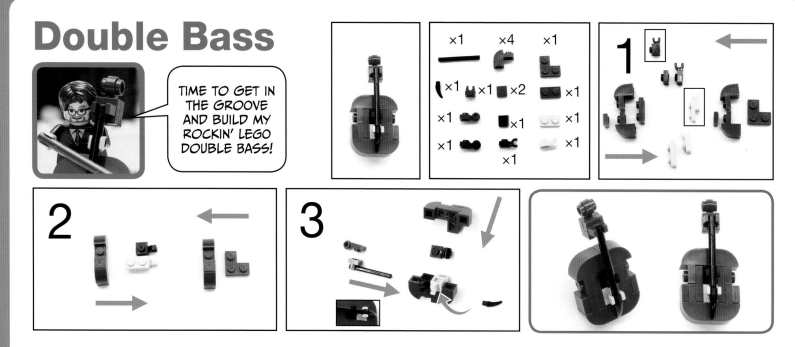

Croatian National Theatre

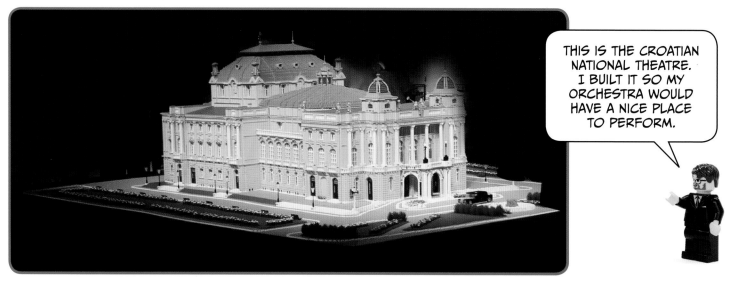

BUILDING JOURNAL

Matija's professional LEGO work is so inspiring! He can build pretty much anything he sets his mind to.

As a LEGO Certified Professional, he builds a lot of models for a wide client base. He told me it is very important to be able to understand clients' needs and pay close attention to your parts budget. Keeping a model simple and retaining the iconic details can be challenging, but the end result is well worth it. Time management and a good solid plan will get you far. His passions for music and LEGO model building go hand in hand. He has shown me there are no limits to turning what you love to do into a career!

177

Rise of the Brickzards

Destruct-o-Lux

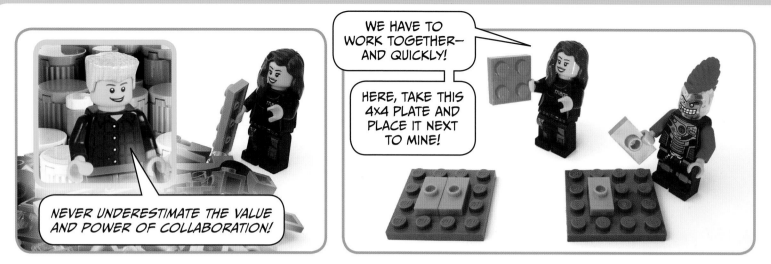

Transport-o-Lux Deluxe

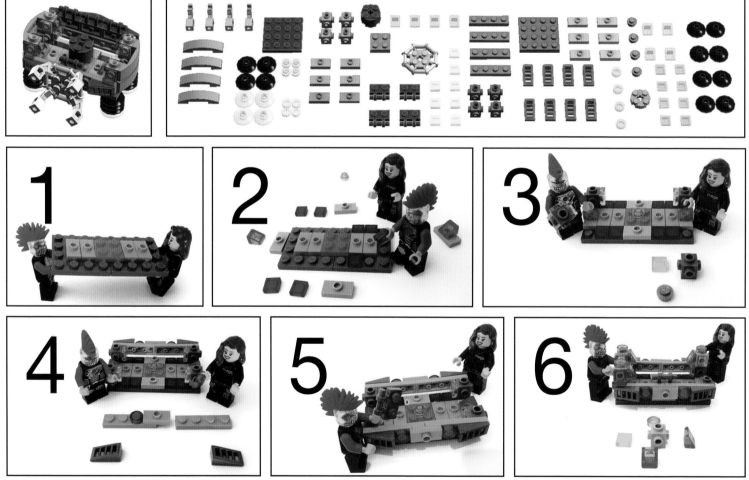

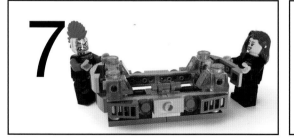
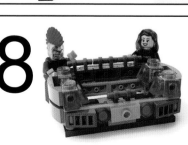

Frilled Brickzard

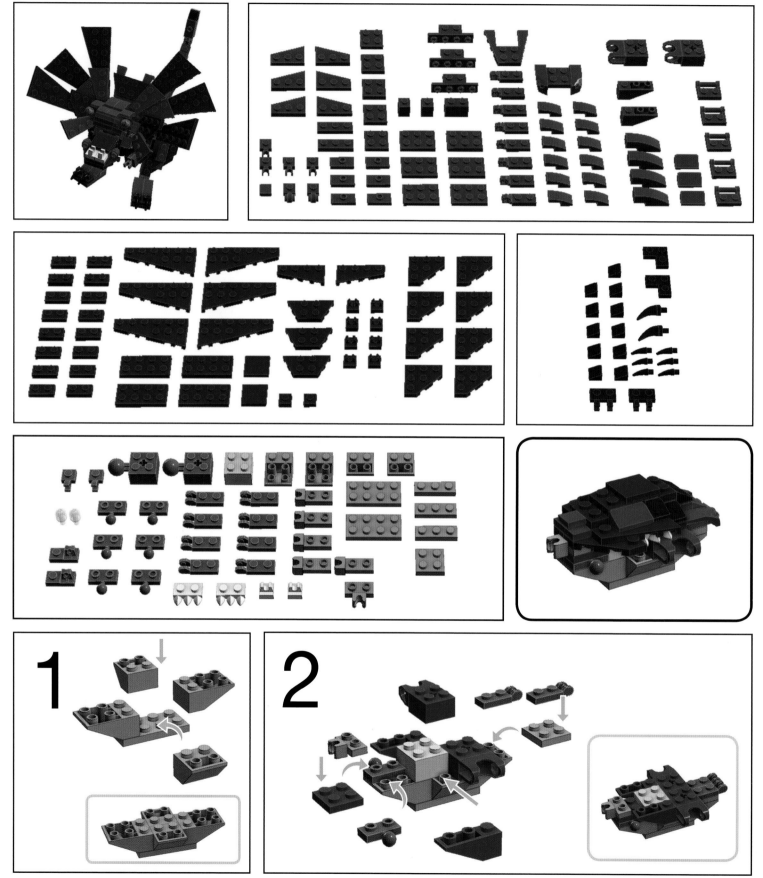

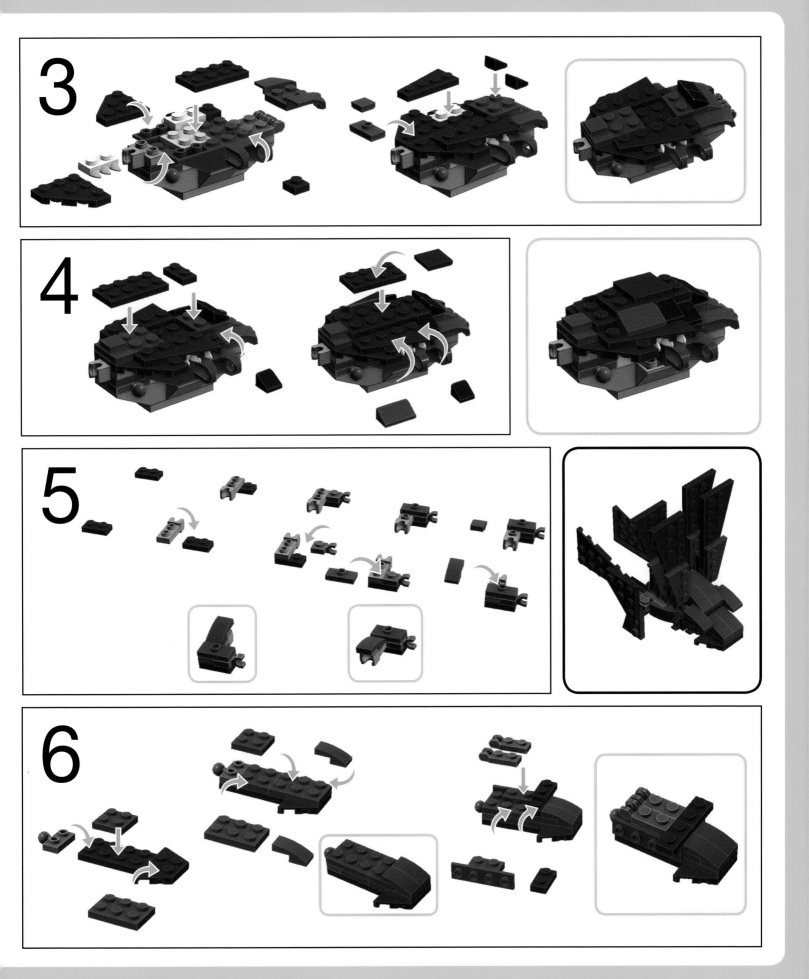

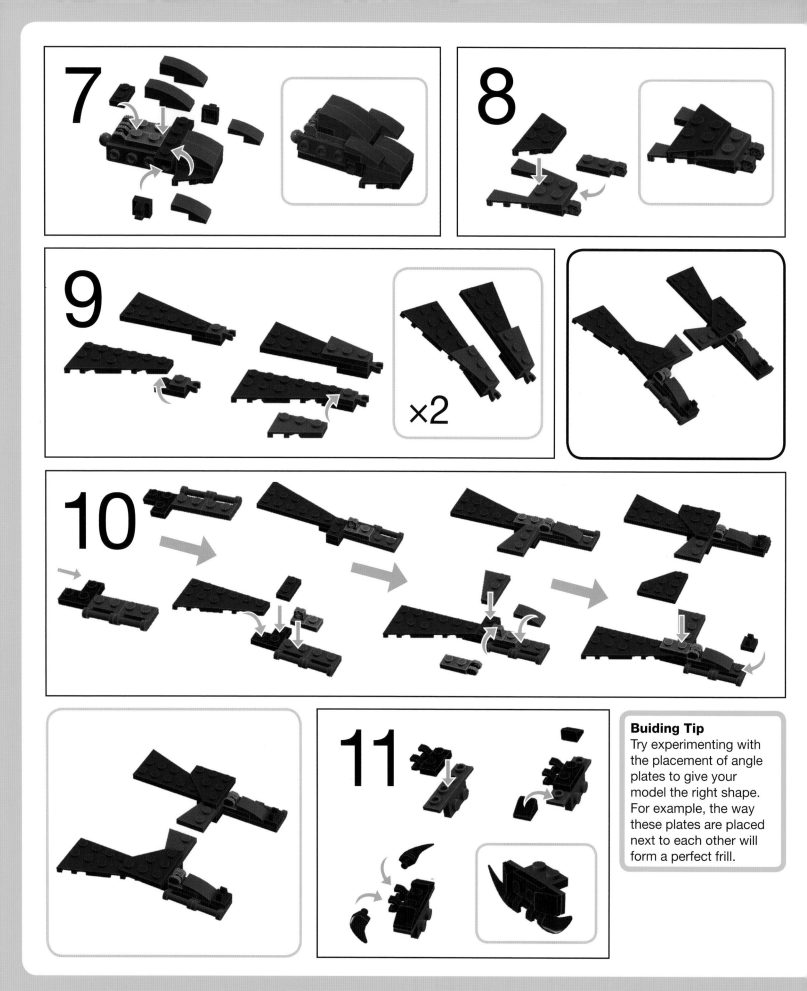

Buiding Tip
Try experimenting with the placement of angle plates to give your model the right shape. For example, the way these plates are placed next to each other will form a perfect frill.

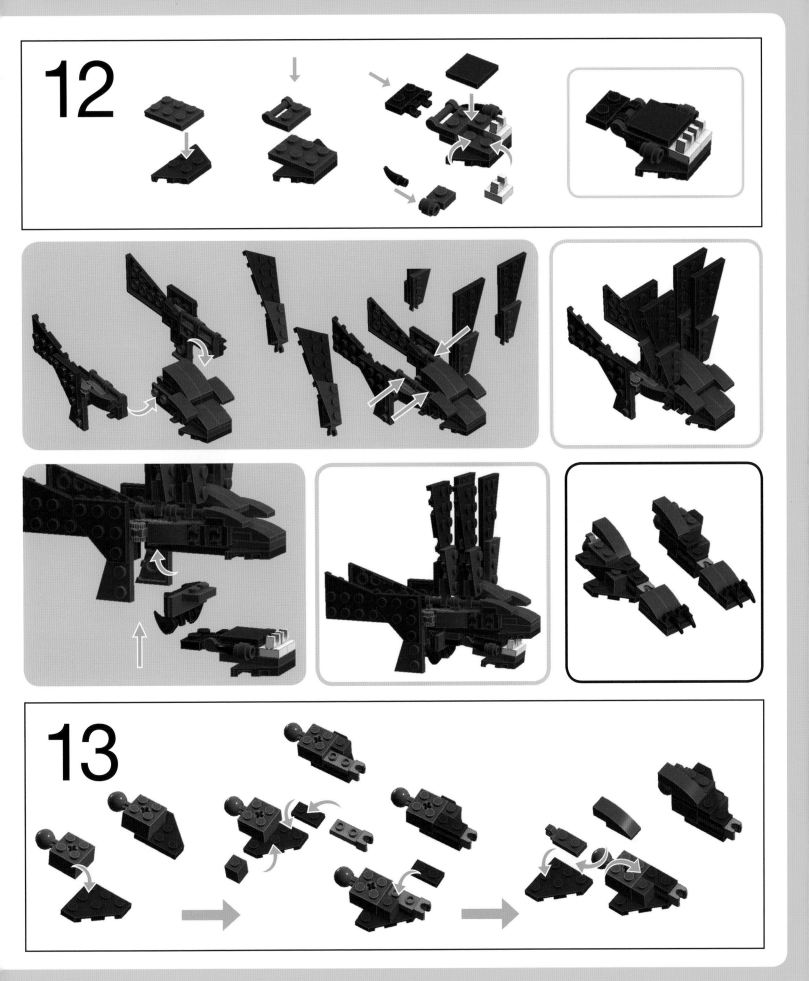

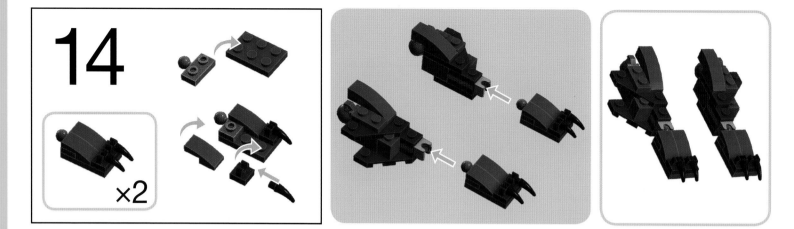

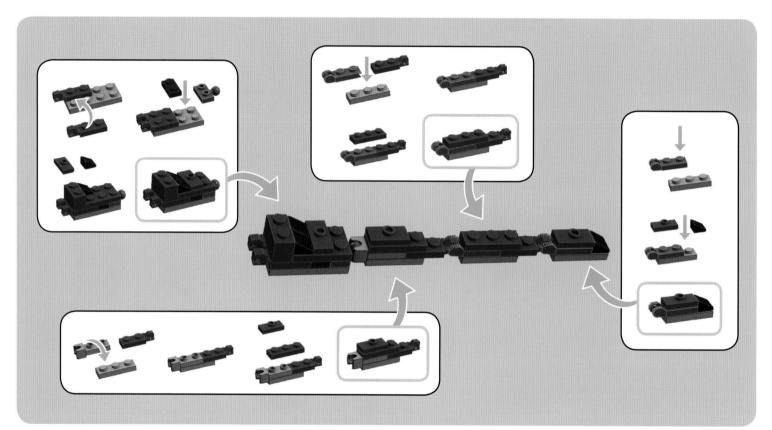

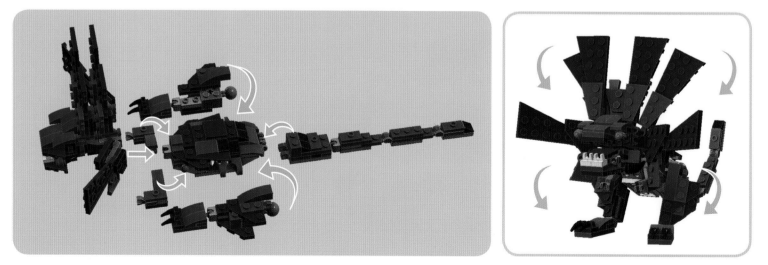

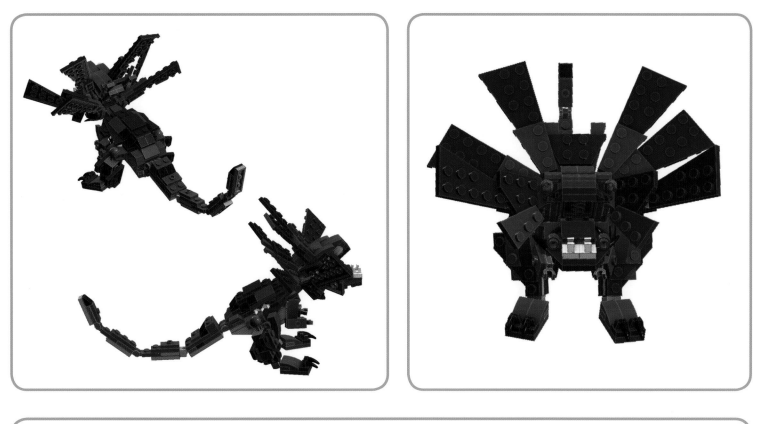

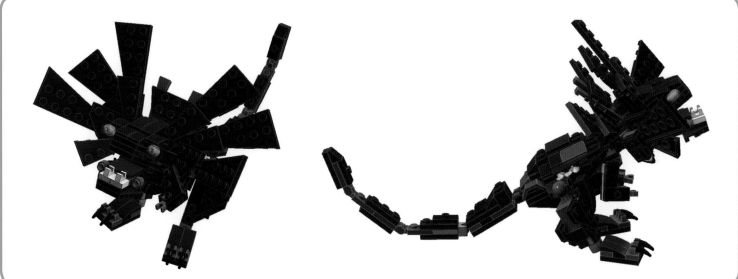

BUILDING JOURNAL

A giant beastie that eats LEGO bricks?! Oh dear!

I find these Frilled Brickzards quite scary, but at the same time, I'm oddly fascinated by them. Perhaps it is because of my affinity for scaled creatures. The Brickzards seem to be intelligent communicators that have a pack mentality. In any case, it is quite clear that ingenuity and collaboration is the only way out of this situation!

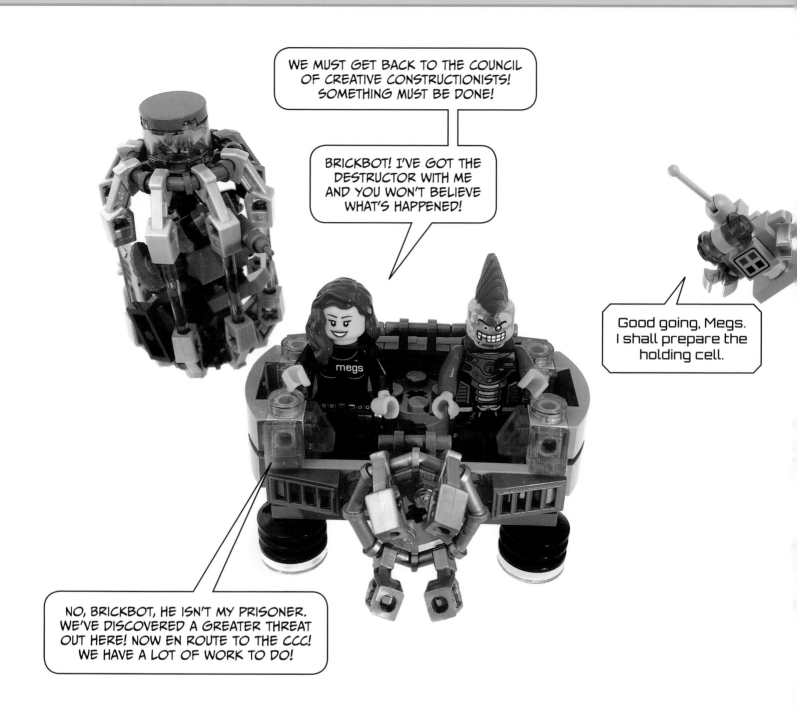

The adventure continues...

Megan H. Rothrock

1

Nickname: megs/megzter
Profession: Toy Designer and Author
Nationality: American
Website: www.flickr.com/photos/megzter/

The LEGO® Adventure Book series is dedicated to all the dreamers and lovers of LEGO building with LEGO bricks around the world.

Thank you to all of the creative and brilliant featured builders!

Featured Builders

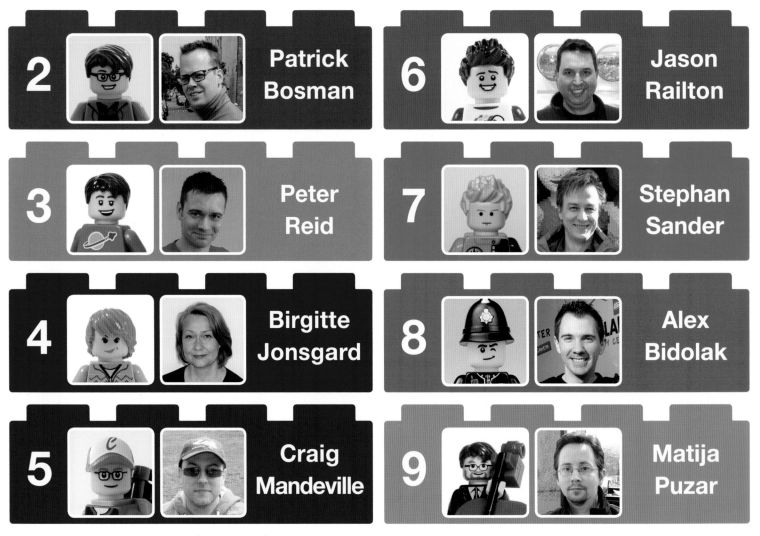

2 Patrick Bosman

3 Peter Reid

4 Birgitte Jonsgard

5 Craig Mandeville

6 Jason Railton

7 Stephan Sander

8 Alex Bidolak

9 Matija Puzar

Join the LEGO Adventure Book community!

Facebook: *www.facebook.com/LegoAdventureBook/*
Flickr: *www.flickr.com/groups/2021445@N23/*
No Starch: *www.nostarch.com/legoadventure3/*

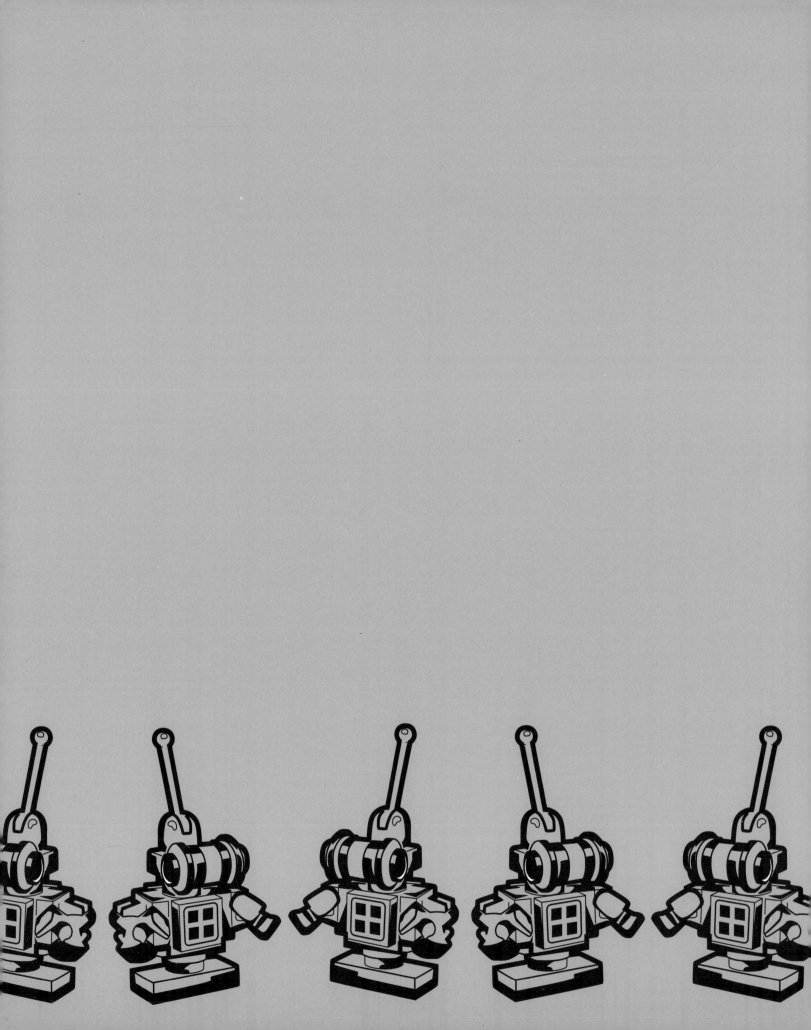